"*The Power of Validation* is an immensely valuable book about helping our children feel worthy and valued. It is written with a compassionate conviction, backed by empirical evidence, and illustrated with vivid anecdotes. The wisdom of these words touches us not only as parents, but as humans longing to be validated for who we are. What greater gift could we possibly give our children than to lovingly recognize, accept, and validate their lives?"

—Brent LoCaste-Wilken, LCSW, CEAP, adjunct professor at the University of Houston Graduate College of Social Work

"Validation is the number-one skill in improving relationships with children of all ages, partners, family members, and even colleagues in the workplace. *The Power of Validation* by Karyn D. Hall and Melissa H. Cook details how and why each of us should master this powerful skill. This is a must-read book for parents and teachers of young children, and most definitely a refreshing and creative reading experience for all who value rewarding relationships!"

—Jim and Diane Hall, family educators for the National Alliance on Mental Illness and the National Education Alliance for Borderline Personality Disorder

"*The Power of Validation* is a veritable roadmap for parents. The destination charted on this roadmap is the creation of a child who has healthy self-esteem and can face the slings and arrows of daily life with confidence and resilience. Parents and those who are anticipating the challenges of parenthood will richly benefit from spending some time with this superb new book."

—Glen O. Gabbard, MD, The Gabbard Center in Houston, TX

"Never before has a book about parenting tackled the seemingly simple topic of validation. In this groundbreaking guide, the authors reveal the amazing power of validation in the development of a strong and healthy child. As we learn how validation galvanizes identity and bolsters self-esteem, we also learn about the wreckage of invalidating environments—a delicate subject compassionately addressed by the authors at every turn. In short, a must-read for every parent, a treasure for anyone wanting to boost their emotional intelligence, and a string of pearls for mental health clinicians of every stripe."

—Kimberly A. Arlinghaus, MD, associate professor of psychiatry at Baylor College of Medicine in Houston, TX

"*The Power of Validation* is a welcome addition to the field. It takes the construct of validation to a practical level, providing exercises that help readers go beyond the written word. The audience for the book should include parents as well as mental health professionals, given its important focus and user-friendly approach."

—Perry D. Hoffman, PhD, president of the National Education Alliance for Borderline Personality Disorder

"In *The Power of Validation*, Karyn D. Hall and Melissa H. Cook provide a roadmap for building the right emotional foundation for your child's life success. Recognizing and accepting your child's feelings is an easy addition to your parenting skill set as well as an elegantly simple and powerful antidote to the pressure of figuring out how to raise competent, successful children."

—Kay M. Albrecht, PhD, early childhood teacher educator at Innovations in Early Childhood Education, Inc., in Houston, TX

"As a pediatrician and mother, I have read hundreds of parenting books, but this one boils it all down into one easy concept. I have found this book to be an invaluable parenting tool in my own home as well as in my practice. If you've grappled with issues such as bullying and peer pressure, this book provides a tried and true solution that will bring harmony to your relationship with your children and give you a sense of competence in your role as a parent. The authors' down-to-earth writing style makes the hugely powerful concept of validation relevant and effective for all parents. It is truly a fresh perspective on parenting."

> —Pamela R. Carmain, MD, FAAP, clinical associate professor in the
> Department of Pediatrics at Baylor College of Medicine in
> Houston, TX

"Validation makes us feel like we matter. It makes us feel like our feelings are not wrong. With validation, we have a stronger and closer bond with our parents."

> —Stuart, age 15, David, age 13, and Caroline, age 11

"*The Power of Validation* is a welcome resource for any parent, teacher, or clinician who wants to optimize their effectiveness in contributing to any young person's emotional development. Hall and Cook have written an easy-to-read, compassionate book that describes the importance, process, and challenges of validation with clear instructions, examples, and practice exercises that can teach and hold the interest of a family member or professional at any level of education or experience. We will definitely refer both family members and colleagues to this book as a tool for teaching the power of validation to promote emotional stability, self-esteem, and effective collaboration in any young person."

> —Lois W. Choi-Kain, MD, clinical instructor in psychiatry and
> director of the Gunderson Residence of McLean Hospital

"*The Power of Validation* is a must-read, no matter how old your child may be. What an eye-opening experience it is to practice validation on a regular basis. The struggles and conflicts disappear and compassion and love emerge. It's a win-win for parent and child and helps parents build a stronger, healthier relationship with their children. I wish I had these tools when my kids were toddlers, but it's never too late to start. Even my seventeen-year-old daughter is much more willing to communicate and share her feelings the more I practice validating her. Thank you for writing this book and empowering me to make a change in the way I listen and respond to my kids."

—Michelle Fredricks, mother of two in Houston, TX

"Quite simply, this is one of the most powerful and effective parenting books I own. It is an invaluable tool for raising emotionally balanced kids."

—Kristine J. Madorsky, MEd, LPC, teacher and elementary school counselor in Houston, TX

"Validating our children does not always come naturally, but is a true gift that we can learn to give to the people we love. I have witnessed immediate healing results when I use this concept with my children, my husband, and in my other relationships."

—Jennifer A. Kearns, MEd, parent and teacher

"Wow—it truly works! If you are like me, an exhausted, busy parent, you are constantly looking for ways to help your family that don't take too much time. This book gently reminds the reader why it is so important that our children feel validated to ensure they are emotionally stable and self-reliant. The best recommendation comes from my children, who now share that they feel more confident in their ability to make decisions."

—Jana Ames, managing director of an international consulting company and mother of twins

THE POWER OF
VALIDATION

Arming Your Child Against Bullying, Peer Pressure, Addiction, Self-Harm & Out-of-Control Emotions

KARYN D. HALL, PhD
MELISSA H. COOK, LPC

New Harbinger Publications, Inc.

Publisher's Note

Distributed in Canada by Raincoast Books

Copyright © 2012 by Karyn D. Hall and Melissa H. Cook
New Harbinger Publications, Inc.
5674 Shattuck Avenue
Oakland, CA 94609
www.newharbinger.com

Cover design by Amy Shoup; Acquired by Catharine Meyers; Edited by Nelda Street

---

Library of Congress Cataloging-in-Publication Data

Hall, Karyn D.
 The power of validation : arming your child against bullying, peer pressure, addiction, self-harm, and out-of-control emotions / Karyn D. Hall and Melissa H. Cook.
    p. cm.
 Includes bibliographical references.
 ISBN 978-1-60882-033-7 (pbk.) -- ISBN 978-1-60882-034-4 (pdf e-book)
 1. Emotions in children. 2. Identity (Psychology) in children. 3. Validation therapy. 4. Parental acceptance. 5. Parenting--Psychological aspects. I. Cook, Melissa H. II. Title.
 BF723.E6H35 2011
 155.4'124--dc23

                              2011027874

14   13   12

10   9   8   7   6   5   4   3   2   1

First printing

To my children, who remind me daily of the importance of validation.

To my husband, Douglas. I would not be a therapist, much less an author, without your support.

—Melissa Cook

For my mom and Chris. They know why.

For Melissa, who had an idea one day. Look what happened.

—Karyn Hall

Contents

Foreword

I first started learning about validation as a part of dialectical behavior therapy (DBT). DBT is a treatment that was created for suicidal people who were emotionally and behaviorally out of control. Marsha Linehan, PhD., who created DBT, realized that one of the problems in treating these people was that when she would try to tell them things that would solve their life problems, their emotions got more intense. As the emotions went up, the clients would stop participating in the therapy sessions. The emotional clients would no longer be able to process new information or recall old information, and ultimately, the clients would either verbally attack the therapist or leave the therapy session. There needed to be a mechanism for bringing emotional arousal down in session. Dr. Linehan started adding specific, concrete validation to her work with emotional clients. When clients started having increased emotion and shutting down or attacking, Marsha would move in and validate some aspect of the client's responses. When she did this well, the client's emotion would go down and the therapy session would continue.

As validation was developed, Dr. Linehan began to realize that there were specific times and ways to validate the experience of the client. She realized that she couldn't just agree with someone who was distressed, and she realized that if she immediately argued against a problematic response, she would inadvertently invalidate the person. For example, when someone you care about says "I am a bad person,"-the natural response is to say, "No, you're not." This statement could actually invalidate the emotional person and cause emotion to further increase. From this knowledge arose the whens and hows of validation.

When DBT was first in development, the thought was that only emotionally sensitive, suicidal mental health clients needed validation. Over the years, however, we have realized that we *all* need validation. If my husband comes home from work and has had a bad day, he will be emotional. If I move right in to telling him what he should have done differently, he will be more emotional. If I stop, listen well, and validate his experience of the day, his emotions will go down. Then, if I want to give him feedback, he will be open to it.

It didn't take long for mental health practitioners to realize that validation is a key to effective parenting. Karyn Hall and Melissa Cook have taken what DBT therapists everywhere have found to be effective in lowering emotions and applied it to parenting. They have provided a foundation to understand validation and its the steps and strategies, and they offer ways to troubleshoot your validation efforts.

Karyn and Melissa are excellent therapists. I have been working with Karyn since 2003 and Melissa since 2005. I know their competence in DBT. I have referred clients to both of them for years and have been so impressed with Karyn that when my partners and I founded the Treatment Implementation Collaborative, LLC to work with therapists, clients, and family members, she was one of the first people we asked to be a trainer/supervisor for the company. Melissa was just finishing school when we began monthly supervision meetings. She has been extremely effective at working with the most difficult, emotionally out-of-control clients. She is passionate and compassionate about her work and about her children. I have watched Melissa develop the skills for validation into parenting skills and heard stories of the effectiveness of validation in parenting her children.

The Power of Validation doesn't say that validation is easy or that it comes naturally. Parents love their children, and when children are distressed, parents want to solve the problem. It is human nature to just jump in and try to fix the situation--to get your kid to quit cryingor get your kid to listen.

Validation requires stepping back a little, finding some wisdom and understanding in your child's responses, and communicating that understanding. Sometimes, validation feels unnatural and counterintuitive. Let Karyn and Melissa show you--through their teaching, real-life examples, and practices--how to increase the validation that you use with your children and decrease the emotional chaos in your family.

I am very excited about *The Power of Validation* and know you will find it helpful.

—Shari Manning, Ph.D.

Acknowledgments

We would like to thank the countless people who supported us during the process of writing this book. Thanks are due to not only our families but also our friends and colleagues in the Houston community. While there are too many people to list by name, special thanks must specifically be given to Chris Meisenhalder, who has supported us with enthusiasm; Douglas Cook, for his constant support and help with reads and rereads; Dr. Shari Manning, for all of the wisdom she has shared with us; Dr. Pam Carmain, who passionately encouraged us to turn our ideas into a book; and Kris Madorsky, our parent editor, who took her job seriously and validated us in the process.

A very special thank-you, in particular, goes to Stuart, David, and Caroline Cook, Melissa's children, who were the most validated during our process of writing this book. The idea to develop validation into a parenting concept came about through Melissa's interactions with her own children. They have responded in an immeasurable way, and we are grateful to them for serving as our own research subjects.

Thanks also must go to our clients. Much of our experience is based on issues and challenges identified by the patients in our clinical practice. We are eternally grateful for their confidence in us as clinicians, and they should know that we learn from them every day and appreciate their faith in us!

Last, we would like to thank New Harbinger Publications for taking a chance on a couple of new authors who had the idea to share with others how to become a validating parent.

Introduction

Because we are passionate about teaching validation and feel strongly about sharing information about it with parents, it is a calling for us, as therapists. We wholeheartedly believe that validation is one of the most important things you, as a parent or caregiver, can give your child to help him thrive and become a fully functioning adult. This book will teach you how to validate.

Validation is important for helping children develop autonomy and a secure sense of self, and it may help prevent emotional problems or even emotional disorders. Knowing how to validate your children will improve your relationships with them, because feeling heard and understood strengthens the bond and attachment they feel toward you. Validation also improves the relationships children eventually form in their adult lives. A validated child is one who feels confident that she can express who she is and how she feels to her parents with complete acceptance without fear of judgment. Imagine the freedom in that.

We believe that validation is key to children's success and development. We believe that invalidating children can lead to serious emotional issues. It will also teach your child to be comfortable with his own emotions. Imagine the child who comes to you upset that his two front teeth stick out in a way that makes him look and feel awkward. Although it's hard to hear that your child is unhappy, telling him that he has no reason to be upset about his teeth is an example of invalidation. Parents often do this because they don't want their child to be upset. Accepting the way your child feels about his teeth is validation. It sounds easy, but it's not. After reading this book, you will gain insight into how to implement a validating strategy into your parenting style.

Validation: A Simple but Powerful Idea

On the surface, validation is a simple concept. The idea just doesn't sound complicated or new enough to make a difference in the very difficult task of parenting. But sometimes the most powerful ideas are the simplest ones. Take, for instance, washing your hands to stop the spread of germs. How simple is that? Robert Fulghum (2004) wrote that much of the information we need in life is taught in kindergarten, such as to clean up our own messes, share everything, and avoid taking what isn't ours. The wisdom in these simple ideas serves all ages and is relevant in the most complex situations. That's how it is with validation.

Validation is a powerful concept. Researchers believe that life experiences, especially experiences with other people, affect the way the developing brain functions (Siegel 1999). For this reason and because validation improves relationships, using validation effectively and consistently will enhance your child's developing brain. In addition, experts on the psychology of happiness have found that relationships with others are one of the keys to happiness (Seligman 2002), so the tendency of validation to enhance relationships will contribute to your child's overall happiness. Because validation helps your child build a secure sense of self, it arms your child against bullies, peer pressure, the need for girls to focus on appearance to attract boys, and the risk of failure. Validation can be one of the best gifts you give your child.

That's a huge payoff for using such a simple skill. What's the catch? Although a simple concept to understand, validation is more difficult to practice, especially under stress. Reading this book will give you an intellectual understanding of validation, but to get the most out of this book, it's important to practice. Most skills require practice, whether this means playing an instrument, speaking a foreign language, cooking, or dancing. While you might be tempted to skip the exercises in this book, doing so could limit the benefits you gain as a parent. For validation to work and for your child to benefit, practice is essential.

Who Could Benefit from This Book

Validation is a skill that can enhance all interpersonal exchanges. Our focus is on parents of young children, aged four to twelve. We chose this age group because of the importance of validation to emotional development during those years. This book could also be helpful for parents of children with a problem such as anxiety disorder or depression. Learning to implement validation while parenting children with special needs could be particularly useful.

This book also could be useful to adults who do not know how to validate themselves or to parents of adult children who have difficulty managing their emotions.

Why We Wrote This Book

We wrote this book out of sheer passion, desire, and a calling to spread the word of validation, a concept that has come to mean far more to us now than we ever thought possible. We hope that as you read this book, you will grow to appreciate this concept as as much as we do.

Some might ask, "Why another parenting book?" Surely, with the number of books on the shelves, there's little else to add to the field, right? We disagree. This is the best parenting tool you can use: the simplest, the least expensive, and the one that will cultivate the most peace in your home!

For over thirty years, Karyn has worked with children, teens, and adults who suffer the agony of being indecisive; disliking themselves; and feeling left out, not good enough, and unsure of their identities. She has also worked with countless people suffering from depression and anxiety disorders to the extent that they couldn't leave their homes or were suicidal. Karyn has sat with parents of teens and adult children who had committed suicide and has listened to the frustrations of youth with eating disorders who wanted to live their lives but couldn't stop bingeing, purging, or restricting food. Hoping to make a difference, Karyn is convinced that people's quality of life is connected to the quality of their relationships.

Besides having experienced the power of validation in her work as a therapist trained in dialectical behavior therapy, Karyn has used validation effectively in her personal life. For Karyn, teaching the concept of validation is a way to help children grow into emotionally healthy adults and to help them develop the skills and characteristics necessary to build satisfactory relationships. Most disorders are seen as a combination of biology and environment, and although we cannot change biology, we can improve a child's environment. Validation is a powerful way to do that.

Melissa's perspective comes from being both a therapist and a mother of three. She has trained in validation skills for approximately six years. Most of her clients struggle with emotional disorders, such as anorexia, bulimia, self-harm, and depression. When she saw her clients and their parents become successful in their relationships just by using validation, she realized that these skills would serve as a great parenting tool for all children. With this knowledge, she started applying validation to parenting her own children. She started to see that validating her children's feelings elicited entirely new responses. Just having their feelings validated helped them feel heard, understood, closer to her, and more willing to respond to redirection or discipline, if necessary. Her husband joined her in applying validation when he realized how effective it was.

Through her training in dialectical behavior therapy, Melissa also learned that validation could be just the skill to apply to parenting to foster emotionally healthy adults, which in turn may prevent eating disorders and other emotional disorders that are often exacerbated by a child's environment. One of her parenting goals became to attempt to raise a validated child with a strong sense of self and a strong sense of internal validation. As an adolescent, Melissa developed anorexia and was hopeful that she could prevent this mental illness from negatively affecting her own children. She became so ill from her disease that she almost died. It was at that point that she sought therapy to try to regain the sense of self she had lost in her illness. Her own experience with anorexia, and her desire to prevent it in others, is part of why she was called to create a forum for teaching parents to recognize what an impact validation can have on a child's upbringing.

Melissa is the first to admit that parenting is an incredibly difficult job. No one gives you a manual, and each child is different. Parenting is an even more challenging job when your child has intense emotions that are difficult to deal with. It is through teaching validation to her clients and her family, and in many other forums, that Melissa sees its power. She is confident that as you read further, you will respond positively to the simplicity and effectiveness of validation.

We wrote this parenting book because we believe in the power of validation, and we believe that reading this book will give you some insight into what it's like to raise a validated child.

Points to Ponder

You can expect to learn more and more about validation as you read on and complete the exercises. We believe you will gain a better understanding of the concept of validation and why it is so important. You can also expect to develop a more connected relationship with your child, which in turn will help your child feel more connected with you. You and your family will be healthier emotionally. If you practice validation, you will experience its power for yourself, just as we have.

Get your notebook ready. Intellectually understanding an idea is very different from applying it. You can read about how to build a Web page or make a soufflé, but actually doing it is quite different. True learning involves applying the ideas you have read. We've included many exercises in this book to give you an opportunity to apply the concepts you are learning. We urge you to complete the exercises even if you find them mundane or are tempted to skip them. Think through the advantages to doing the exercises: you will gain a better understanding of what you read, be more likely to remember the ideas discussed, develop validation skills in steps, and be more likely to apply them. You may have other reasons why completing the exercises would be helpful to you. We encourage you to make a commitment now to complete each exercise as you come to it rather than merely read the book straight through.

Chapter 1

Understanding Validation

I n this chapter we explain the basic idea of validation, referencing much of the work of Marsha Linehan (1997). First, let's clarify the concept of validation by sharing a few stories and discussing what validation is and isn't. This is the crux of understanding our validating parenting model.

Validation Stories

You will soon understand validation and work it into your everyday parenting style. Although validation is not easy to implement, your doing so empowers your child to become the fully functioning adult she is meant to be. As you read the following stories, think about what your reaction might have been. Consider what situations would be difficult for you to listen to compassionately, with respect for your child's feelings. Remember, validation is not about whether your child's ideas are right or wrong; it's about how she feels in the particular situation.

• Carter's Story

Carter, a normally sweet-natured seven-year-old who never gives his parents any trouble, is lying on the ground at a theme park, pitching a super-sized tantrum because his mother refuses to buy him a lollipop.

Carter's mother watches, exhausted and embarrassed. Devoted to their family, Carter's parents give their children everything they can without spoiling them. At a popular theme park for a special weekend, the children have been allowed to indulge in many activities. Their hotel offers a man-made lazy river, bike paths, s'mores, movies on the lawn, and room service. The family has spent two full days feeding dolphins, riding roller coasters, watching a killer whale show, swimming, and generally having fun together.

At the end of the second day, the family walks out of the park to end their time there and return to the fabulous hotel. As they exit, Carter asks for a lollipop—not just any lollipop but one that's bigger than his head. At first he asks if he can stop to get one. Being only seven, he doesn't realize that a shuttle bus is waiting to take everyone back to the hotel and that there's a time constraint. When his mother refuses, Carter digs in his heels and demands to get his way. He even claims this will go down in history as the worst day of his life if he doesn't get that lollipop. This easygoing, trouble-free kid throws an unprovoked, implausible tantrum for a lollipop in front of about a hundred guests leaving the park.

Unsure how to respond, his mother notices the following thoughts going through her mind:

You ungrateful child! Look how much you have been given today!

How can you say this is the worst day ever? Look at all the fun you had today!

Get over it! You are not getting that lollipop.

You just don't want the fun to end, but it has to. Think about the fun you'll still have at the hotel when you return.

Wow, you are such a brat! With all that we've given you, I can't believe you're complaining!

Now, realistically, a lollipop at the end of his time at the theme park isn't that much for Carter to ask. The family is on vacation, and his mother can understand that it would be a nice way to wrap up a banner day. But Carter's parents decide to say no. Not only is the shuttle waiting, but also everyone in the family is hot and tired; they want to return to the hotel, shower, and enjoy a family dinner before the children's bedtime. Besides, his parents don't want to raise a child who believes he should get everything he wants.

Carter's mother grows more embarrassed and more frustrated with him, feeling inadequate as a mother. She knows that acting on her own frustration will make things worse. Two tantrums would not be better than one, especially if a grown woman threw one. Carter's mom decides to try some validation strategies she has learned. She kneels down to Carter's level, looks him in the eye, and says, "Carter, I can see that you are really upset that you're not getting this lollipop."

Her son looks at her: "This has been the worst day ever, and I want that lollipop."

His mom bites her tongue, again wanting to say all the things she has been thinking and feeling. Instead she responds, "I can see that you feel this has been the worst day ever because you aren't getting what you want."

Carter calmly replies, "Yes, I'm really sad."

"It makes sense that you are sad. I get it."

Carter then asks again for the lollipop, and his mom replies that they aren't buying any candy, but validates that she understands how much he really wants it. The tantrum ceases, and Carter again states his feelings, stands, and calmly walks out of the theme park. Although still sad, he is at least now managing his feelings effectively. Having his feelings understood and heard rather than argued with helps him accept his disappointment. His mother teaches Carter that what he feels makes sense, that she hears him. Her response does not mean that she agrees with how he feels, just that she agrees that he is allowed to have his feelings.

In our experience, one of the worst things that parents can do to their children is to not allow them to have the feelings that they feel. And one of the hardest things for parents to do is to allow their children to have feelings that are not all perfect and happy. Validation means allowing your children to feel negative feelings and allowing those feelings to be heard. Again, you won't always agree with how they feel but the point is to not argue.

• John's Story

John, an easygoing twelve-year-old, is excited to go on an overnight trip with his seventh-grade class. While he gets along well with all of his classmates, he has selected a few to be his roommates on the trip. Although his mother is a bit uneasy about his trip, she hopes things will go well for John. When her son calls her late in the evening of the first day, John's mom is surprised, because her son never actually calls unless it's something major; he usually sends a text message instead. John tells his mother he is "pissed off" because he didn't get placed in a room with the group he had selected. Although the emotion he expresses is anger, his mom picks up on how upset and vulnerable John feels. She sits and listens to John rant and rave with nothing positive at all to say about his day, which included a trip to a theme park and three museums with all of his buddies. While his mom knows he must have had some fun, it's crucial at this point to listen to him as he conveys his upset feelings. As John finishes his frustrated rant, his mom lets the line go quiet. It goes so quiet that John has to ask her what she thinks. His mother pauses and responds, "That just sucks. Such a bummer!" This is hard for her to say, because she wants to fix things so her child can be happy, by saying, "Just go to sleep; you are getting up at six in the morning and can hang with your buddies then," or "Wow, you are really spoiled; just get over it and hope for a better tomorrow." While these statements sound reasonable, neither acknowledges John's current view of the world. He is upset and needs the one person he has called, his mother, to hear him. Well, thankfully she does. John's entire emotional tirade defuses, and he says good-bye to his mother and goes to bed. He has been heard, which was all he needed. He did not need her to fix the problem or try to argue away his feelings. He just needed to hear that his emotions were valid, and his mom provided that with validation.

• Emily's Story

It's Emily's birthday. She is turning eleven, and this day is very important to her. In her friend's family, birthdays are always celebrated. All day long Emily waits for her parents to acknowledge her birthday. They do nothing. Finally, when it's clear that they have nothing planned, she asks them if they forgot. "No," her dad says, "I remembered." Shocked, Emily asks why they didn't plan a celebration, even just a little one. He responds, "I didn't think you wanted to celebrate your birthday anymore. That's what you said last year. Aren't you getting a little too old for that sort of thing?" Emily is crushed. She feels like a child in a grown-up body, and her feelings are invalidated. It does not matter that in her family, elaborate birthday parties are thrown only for small children. She wanted a celebration, so her request for a party was important to her. Being told she shouldn't want a party feels hurtful, even when she knows her parents haven't meant to hurt her feelings. A simple correction would make this experience different. If her father validated her hurt feelings, she would likely respond differently. A statement like "I see that you are hurt. I didn't realize this was important to you" would go a long way to help Emily feel better understood and less upset.

After reading these example stories, you are probably starting to get a grasp on validation. You can use validation with your spouse, coworkers, or neighbors, and it can be beneficial in almost any relationship. As a parent, starting to implement some of these strategies will chart the course for incredible relationships with your children as they grow into adolescence and adulthood. Now we'll discuss what validation is and is not.

What Validation Is

As it is normally used, "validation" seldom refers to children or parenting styles. We validate parking, we validate ourselves for a job well done, we validate our achievements, but we do not naturally validate our children. *Validation* is the recognition and acceptance that your child has feelings and thoughts that are true and real to him regardless of logic or whether it makes sense to anyone else.

To validate is to offer acceptance and feedback about the other person's reality in a nonjudgmental way. To validate is to acknowledge and accept a person's individual identity. When you validate a child, you allow her to share her feelings and thoughts without your judgment. You also reassure her, without questioning or disapproving, that her feelings are neither right nor wrong but are, in fact, her feelings. You show that you still accept her after she has shared her feelings, and you let her know that you respect her perception of the situation at that moment. You allow her to feel heard, acknowledged, understood, and accepted—not ridiculed or abandoned—based on the feelings she has expressed. Through validation, children learn that they are accepted and loved, no matter what feelings or thoughts they have. All the money in the world can't buy for your child what validation can.

Validation helps children own a deep sense of acceptance and normalcy. Think what protection that would provide: if children had an absolute sense of acceptance and normalcy, bullies would lose their power, girls would not assess their value through attracting boys regardless of the cost, and teens would not need to escape reality through substance abuse. Developing a 100-percent sense of self-acceptance and normalcy is impossible due to biological factors and interaction with adults who are unfamiliar with the power of validation. Though you can't reach a perfect sense of acceptance and normalcy, you can enhance those characteristics and help reduce your child's insecurity, feelings of being different, and need to please others.

Validation is not a new concept. Most therapies for emotional disorders include some form of validation. Often parents believe they are already validating their children when, in fact, they are merely praising, supporting, or giving unconditional love. Validation is different. When we speak at schools about validating parenting, parents request more and more information on the topic. Once they understand the concept, parents seem to recognize its value and are eager to know how they can apply it to their parenting skills. We hear many painful stories from parents who remember being invalidated as children and understand firsthand how that invalidation affected their lives.

We learned about validation from Marsha Linehan (1993), who developed a therapy called *dialectical behavior therapy* (DBT), which applies validation in a specific way. Linehan believes that repeated invalidation of another person's thoughts and feelings can cause more problems in emotional development than you could imagine. Simply telling a child that what he feels is "crazy" could be more damaging to the child than expected. As part of her research, Linehan learned that balancing acceptance of her client with encouragement to change was critical for therapy to be effective with her target population. Having found it to be a key tool for acceptance, Linehan (ibid.) defines validation as communicating to people that their responses make sense and are understandable within their current life contexts or situations.

As defined by *Webster's Online Dictionary* (www.websters-online-dictionary.org), "to validate" is to make valid, substantiate, or confirm. Validating children is simply confirming for them that their feelings, thoughts, and appropriate actions are valid. It's that simple.

Nonverbal Validation

Validation can be nonverbal. With infants, much of validation is through body motions and touch. John Bowlby described how a person's earliest anxiety is related to being insecurely held (Holmes 1993). A mother can hold a child with confidence or with fear and uncertainty. Facial expressions, posture, hand motions, voice tone, gaze, and speed of movement can all communicate emotion. In fact, communication of emotions through facial expressions is universal. What looks happy in Texas also looks happy in Nepal!

Nonverbal communication is powerful. Most of the time, a person will believe nonverbal over verbal communication. If you tell an upset friend that you have all the time in the world to listen to her but keep checking your watch while she is talking, your friend will believe your behavior over your words. Parents use nonverbal communication that their children understand well; for example, most parents give their children a certain look when they are upset. Remember your mother's warning face or her "you're in so much trouble, you'll never get out of it" face? We do!

If you give these nonverbal signals when appropriate, there's no issue. It's important for children to learn about nonverbal social cues.

However, sometimes the validating words are spoken, but the nonverbal cues say something entirely different. Consider this example: Eleven-year-old Carly tells her mother that she no longer wants to play piano—that she hates her teacher, hates practicing, and would rather join the soccer team. Her mother responds with a frustrated look, "Sometimes learning to play music is difficult, and new activities look more exciting and fun. Hating your teacher and hating practicing are pretty serious problems. What's going on?" These are good words, but her mother's facial expression says, "Here we go again," negating her words. Expressing your own frustration may be difficult to resist, and your emotions may seep out in the form of body language. It's classic to respond, "Fine," with a disgusted, angry, or stony look. Everyone knows that means you don't really agree, right? The true message comes through loud and clear.

People can experience validation through words, nonverbal signals, and shared attention to events or objects in the world. As a whole, these experiences may foster the healthy development of a child's mind (Siegel 1999). That is quite impressive for a simple interpersonal interaction tool!

What Validation Is Not

Validation is often combined with other responses, such as teaching, informing, redirecting, encouraging, distracting, or solving problems, but it's not the same as those ways of communicating. Most often, validating a child's feelings, thoughts, sensations, or appropriate actions should be done first, before using other responses. In our experience, parents are usually more comfortable with, and know the value of, giving information, comforting, and solving problems with their children, and they overlook the importance of validating. They may also confuse it with other concepts, such as praise or encouragement. Thus parents often think they are validating their children when they are not.

In teaching validating parenting, we've learned that one of the biggest misconceptions is that many parents believe validation means letting their children do whatever they want to do. This is such a common misconception that parents sometimes dismiss validating parenting without learning what it is. We assure you that validating parenting does not mean lack of discipline.

It Is Not Permissive Parenting

Validating parenting does not mean you let your children do whatever they want or allow them to be free of rules, boundaries, or responsibilities. It means that they have rules and boundaries but their feelings are validated. You do not have to agree with your children. Validating parents set boundaries with their children and employ validating discipline.

Take, for example, the child who doesn't want to go to school. We know there will be days when your children will want to stay home from school. We all had those days as kids! As a parent, you validate that your children do not want to go, perhaps because there's a test that day and it's hard for them to go to school when they're afraid or tired. But you are clear that staying home from school is not an option. Don't validate what is not valid. The feeling of not wanting to go to school is valid, but the behavior of staying home from school is not. Feelings are separate from actions. Feelings are not wrong; they just are—but actions can be wrong.

Validating anger does not mean that there's no consequence for yelling or throwing something. In fact, validating feelings without accepting inappropriate action teaches the child not to allow her feelings to control her and not to act impulsively. To teach a child that she is allowed to be angry is extremely healthy, but to teach her not to respond inappropriately in anger is even better. Helping a child learn ways to appropriately express anger is the best option. Both the feeling and its appropriate expression are important, and you can validate both.

Again, validating the feeling or thought does not mean accepting inappropriate action. A young boy may be so enraged at his friend that he wants to punch him in the face. Physically attacking his friend would be wrong, but the feelings associated with his urges are not. This is an important distinction to make when validating. Validate the feeling, not inappropriate actions. Many parents would be angry with their child for merely having an aggressive thought and punish him accordingly, especially if the child is a boy. The thing to remember is that he did not follow through on it; he just felt it and was not wrong for his feelings. The feeling is actually quite normal.

Although validation is separate from discipline, discipline is still important. As a matter of fact, although it's hard to carry out, in order to be an effective parent, you have to provide effective discipline. Because you understand how your child can be angry enough to throw something doesn't mean there isn't a consequence for the action. Having the feeling is normal. We all get angry, but acting on feelings in a destructive way is not acceptable and has consequences.

Children do not plot ways to stress out their parents, break all the rules, and wreak havoc. They do not wish to be aggressive, lie, break things, or make you totally miserable—at least not unless they are really angry with you! They would like to have a peaceful, safe family life in which they feel loved. Often their behavior is about feeling unloved, unaccepted, or unsafe. "Safe," for children, often means feeling solidly connected to their parents or caregivers (secure attachment).

Sometimes children's tears, temper tantrums, and aggression are a result of being overwhelmed with feelings that they don't know how to manage. For a child who is neurologically sensitive, physical sensations can be overwhelming. The idea of having to endure socks that itch or a bothersome seam all day can be unbearable, and when others don't understand, the child is torn between her own experience and the impressions of others. Sometimes children can't label their feelings, perhaps because they are too overwhelmed to think clearly or are still learning how to name their feelings.

Validating discipline takes these factors into consideration. When you validate a child's feelings, perhaps especially when they make no sense to you, the child is more likely to let you know what makes him feel less loved, less accepted, less important, or otherwise unsafe. Then you have an opportunity to deal with the real issue.

It's your job as a parent to understand how much stimulation your child can effectively manage. Asking repeatedly, "Why do you always hit someone when we go to birthday parties?" is invalidating. But that thought is your cue to step back, identify the problem, and work on solutions. In the case of an overstimulated child, the most effective discipline may be prevention. Perhaps Amy is threatened by the number of children at parties and doesn't feel safe and secure. Maybe she is allergic to sugar. Perhaps she misses you (if you dropped her off or are talking with other parents in another room) and isn't ready to spend time with other children without your being nearby. Preventing or adjusting the situation to manageable levels helps her grow and develop with confidence. Allowing her to continue to struggle will make her wonder what's wrong with her—and frustrate you. Validating discipline means not putting your child in situations she is not ready to manage.

Sometimes, even without underlying issues, children break rules because they want to do what their friends are doing, or they act impulsively, without considering the potential consequences. Children get carried away by having a good time, or they behave inappropriately to impress their friends or simply because that's what they want to do. They will play basketball instead of doing their homework, or they will lie about the broken lamp. Validating discipline means respectfully giving consequences when your child's behavior needs correction. Humiliating and shaming are not part of validating discipline. Every child sometimes breaks rules and makes shocking choices. This behavior is not personal toward you. Your job is to help your children learn that actions have consequences. Sometimes you will want to berate your child in response to his actions, because you are angry or because you want him to feel bad enough to never make such a ridiculous choice again. Your discipline will be more effective if you just provide the consequence without judging your child's character.

Validating discipline is not about what discipline strategies you choose to use; it's about the tone of your discipline and the way you interact with your child. Being angry about your child's choices and behavior is okay—but invalidating your child is not okay.

Validating parenting means recognizing that your child means well most of the time and that misbehavior usually happens for a reason. When the misbehavior is repetitive, the child may be struggling with situations that are difficult for her and for which she may not be developmentally ready. Recognizing this fact and that there are many other reasons why a child might misbehave are part of validating parenting.

It Is Not Inauthentically Parroting Words

Merely restating your child's words without accepting or understanding the feelings behind them is not validating. "I understand that you're angry and think you hate your brother right now," said in a monotonous, bored, or judgmental voice is unhelpful, particularly when you add sarcasm at the end, such as "as always."

Validation means sincerely listening for the meaning of your child's words. Sometimes that takes some searching, and it always takes compassion. It means looking for what is right when your child's words seem so wrong. Of course, you do not want your child to hate her brother, but realistically, we know that sometimes she will, just because he is her brother. It doesn't mean she will always hate him, nor does it mean you are a bad parent. It just means that she has an intense feeling and is not wrong to have that feeling. It is difficult to hear, and it requires setting aside your reactions to allow your children to have their own feelings. Truly listening to your child so that you understand her experience is a form of validation.

It Is Not Being Ruled by Your Child's Emotions

If your daughter says she is sad, responding by asking numerous questions about the sadness and what she needs to be happy is not necessarily validation. You are showing that you care, of course, but you are not letting her know that sadness is okay and doesn't need to be fixed. Nor is validation centering your attention on your child's sadness and trying to distract her with new toys or activities or by finding friends with whom she can play. It is not about trying to fix the problem that's bothering her, for example, by calling another parent to ask that she invite your daughter to her child's birthday party because your daughter is so upset about not being invited. It is not about indulging her and doing whatever is possible to help her be happy again.

Validation is accepting the feeling your child expresses. It is acknowledging the feeling and being okay with it. Your acceptance lets your child know that sadness is normal and can be managed.

It Is Not Paying Undeserved Compliments

If your child is on a soccer team and doesn't play well in a game, saying "You did great!" is not validating. Such statements don't build confidence or encourage a child, because children know the truth. Claiming that something is positive when it is not denies the child's internal experience and does not help him develop a healthy sense of his own judgment and acceptance of the world.

18

Validation would be to state the truth: "It's hard when you don't play as well as you would like," or "It's great that you had such a good time." What you say depends on what the child is experiencing. Perhaps she played well compared to her previous games or just had an off day. Validation is acknowledging the truth of your child's internal experience, that it's normal and okay to not always play your best, be the best player, or do all things perfectly or even well. Validation also allows intense feelings to be released while assuring the child that the next game may offer a whole new opportunity, even if the exact same thing happens.

Reinforcing Undesired Behavior

A behavioral rule in psychology about positive reinforcement states that reinforcing or rewarding any behavior increases the likelihood of that behavior recurring. Most children find attention from their parents reinforcing. Running to your child's side every time he cries increases the likelihood that he will cry in the future. Why doesn't validation increase acting out, giving excuses, or lying?

Part of validation is to acknowledge what's true and authentic. If your child repeatedly cries or teases his sister and it seems to you that he wants your attention, then address this with him. For example, a nine-year-old boy loved to tease his seven-year-old sister, who reacted emotionally every time her brother came near. Part of why the sister reacted so strongly was because her mother did. Because the mother didn't like the teasing, she intervened each time, attending to both the teaser and the teased. The big brother received attention from his mom each time he teased his sister, which reinforced his behavior, causing him to tease more frequently.

The mom realized this after some time and asked her son, "Do you tease your sister because you want attention from me?" The boy actually responded yes. Both mother and son came up with a plan that if he wanted his mom's attention, he just needed to ask. They discussed a way for him to ask for attention directly so that he could receive positive, instead of negative, attention.

It never occurred to the son to ask directly for the attention he wanted, or perhaps he was too embarrassed. His misbehavior had been reinforced, and he had learned how to get his mom's attention in a negative way. The son's true feelings were more about wanting something from his mom than a desire to tease his sister. Acknowledging the true feeling behind the emotions is a key part of validation. Our experience is that when a child's true emotion and experience are validated, the emotion tends to dissipate more quickly, and efforts to express emotions in inappropriate ways cease. Validation reinforces genuine, authentic, and direct communication.

It Is Not Lying

Validating something that is untrue creates as much confusion as invalidating what the child knows is true. If your child is upset that she wasn't invited to a friend's home with other children, validate her feeling (hurt or sad), but do not lie to your child by saying that you are sure that the invitation got lost in the mail or that you are sure that her friend "meant" to invite her but forgot. This will confuse your child. Being truthful and validating will open the door for you to be a safe vessel into which your child can express freely how she feels without any condemnation for it. She will trust you to be truthful.

It Is Not Unconditional Love

Unconditional love means loving your child no matter what. Although unconditional love is critically important in parenting, it is a different concept from validation. Unintended hurt can happen even when unconditional love is present. You can have unconditional love and still invalidate your child's feelings, just as you can have unconditional love and *validate* your child's feelings. When you give unconditional love while invalidating your child's thoughts and feelings, you run the risk of fostering the child's unhealthy dependency on you or others. Unconditional love creates a safe environment, but invalidation teaches the child that he can't make his own decisions and can't keep himself safe, but needs you or someone else to do that. "I love you no matter who else hates you" does not validate the child's loss of a friend. "We've always got each other" does not help the child deal with his emotions about not making the team or about his father's move out of the house. It is actually more confusing to him than simply validating him.

It Is Not Agreeing

Validating what your child thinks or feels is not the same as agreeing. It doesn't mean that you agree at all, not even a little. It just means that you understand that what your child feels is real to her.

For instance, if your child is in a choir and complains about his "horrible" singing, you can acknowledge that how he feels about his singing is okay. Whether or not you agree that your child is not a good singer doesn't matter. You love your child always and unconditionally, and you understand that he believes he is not the all-time perfect choir singer. Unconditional love does not erase your child's feelings, and your response shows that you understand that. Recognizing that your child's view differs from yours—and that while you don't agree, you accept his thoughts as valid—builds his confidence in himself.

Developing Awareness

Have you ever noticed that once you become aware of something, you start to see examples of it everywhere? What was invisible becomes clear, and you register that experience, whereas you didn't previously. Let's work on your awareness of validating behaviors and statements.

Exercise 1.1 Recognizing Validating Statements

Once you understand the concept of validation, the next step is to learn to recognize validating statements when you hear or read them. Read the following statements to practice recognizing validating comments. Mark "V" for each choice that you think is validating:

_____ 1. "Get over yourself!"

_____ 2. "Don't tell me you are upset about losing that old, raggedy backpack. You're too old for mermaid stuff anyway."

_____ 3. "It's hard when your friend has a sleepover with someone else. I'm guessing you feel left out."

_____ 4. "Of course you're scared about going to a new school. Anyone would be nervous."

_____ 5. "I used to feel jealous of my sister too."

_____ 6. "If you ever slam that door again, I'm taking it off the hinges, and you won't have a door."

_____ 7. "As soon as my daughter goes out to play, I want to tell you the funniest thing she did, but don't let her know you know."

_____ 8. "Don't be a baby."

_____ 9. "Hey, want a pizza instead of candy? Pizza would be good."

_____ 10. "I know that you really love that outfit. In my opinion the colors don't go together well."

_____ 11. "Your friends are upset because you're not passing the ball to them when they have open shots. I know because the coach told me they have complained about that."

_____ 12. "Hey, come on—smile. It's not that bad."

_____ 13. "When you scream like that, I have trouble listening to you and don't want to do what you are asking. I know you are upset, and if you could tell me in a lower voice, I could listen and possibly help."

_____ 14. "Don't look at me that way."

_____ 15. "All I do is take care of your needs, and you are so ungrateful."

The validating statements are numbers 3, 4, 5, 10, 11, and 13.

Exercise 1.2   Choosing Validating Statements in Different Situations

1. As a gifted and self-disciplined twelve-year-old middle-school student, Jessica completes her homework and pays attention in class. Her grades throughout the years have always been As. She has a test in Spanish tomorrow and tells you, "I won't do well on this test. I'm so stressed I can't think. I wish I didn't have to go to school; I hate school." She usually says something similar before any test. Check off which of the following you think would be a validating response:

   _____ a. "You'll do fine. You always do. You're very smart."

   _____ b. "It doesn't matter; don't worry about it. One test is not that big of a deal."

   _____ c. "I think it would be a good thing if you did get a lower grade. It's too much pressure on you to never get anything other than As."

   _____ d. "It is a miserable experience to worry about not doing well and to feel scared that you might not know the material. It's probably worse because everyone expects you to do well."

2. Mike has difficulty dribbling the basketball and shoots it when he doesn't have a good shot. He's upset because he wants to play well. How do you respond in a validating manner?

   _____ a. "Just keep practicing. You'll get better."

   _____ b. "It's just a game. The idea is to have fun."

   _____ c. "If you're going to get so upset, maybe you shouldn't play at all."

_____ d. "It hurts when you want something really badly and can't make it happen."

3. Your husband has a temper and sometimes yells at your daughter. She comes to you to complain about his yelling at her for leaving her clothes on the floor. You respond:

    _____ a. "If you'd put your things away, he wouldn't yell at you."

    _____ b. "We all feel lousy when someone yells at us."

    _____ c. "If you didn't misbehave, none of this would happen."

    _____ d. "How many times have you been told to put your clothes away?"

4. You daughter complains to you that her twin sister borrowed her clothes without asking.

    _____ a. You tell her to get over it, that she does it too, so turnabout is fair play.

    _____ b. You tell her you don't want to hear about it; that there are plenty of clothes for both of them.

    _____ c. You suggest that she discuss the problem with her sister.

    _____ d. You say you understand that she's upset and that most people are upset when others borrow things without asking.

5. Your eleven-year-old son calls you from school because he forgot a paper he was supposed to turn in.

    _____ a. "This had better be the last time, because next time I'm not bringing it."

    _____ b. "It's your responsibility. I guess you'll have to figure out how to solve this."

_____ c. "If you'd just get organized, you wouldn't have this problem. I won't always be around to call when you forget things."

_____ d. "You sound worried. I'm sorry, but I am busy and can't get away right now."

6. Your daughter, who is in junior-high school, is crying because the boy she likes doesn't like her.

_____ a. "Honey, you're too young to think about boys anyway."

_____ b. "I've told you about that attitude of yours. Now see where it got you?"

_____ c. "I'm sorry you're hurt. I know you really liked him."

_____ d. "You'll feel better in a few days. These feelings pass."

ANSWERS:

1. _d._ Although several of the statements may be true, only the last one fits the way Jessica feels.

2. _d._ All of the other responses are invalidating ways of saying that Mike shouldn't feel the way he does.

3. _b._ This response does not mean you are angry with your husband. You are just stating the truth about your daughter's feelings. You are also not saying it's okay for her to leave her clothes on the floor.

4. _d._ This response normalizes her feeling without blaming her for the situation. Both a and b are invalidating, because they put the daughter down for how she feels.

5. *d.* Validation in this case doesn't mean changing your schedule to help, especially if this isn't the first time. In refusing help, you can still acknowledge your son's feelings and that he's in a tight spot.

6. *c.* Yes, the feelings will pass, but your daughter needs you to acknowledge that she feels hurt now.

Validating Statements

Take a day or two to listen for validating statements and watch children's reactions to them. Think of someone you regard as skilled in relating to others. Watch this person to see how many of his comments are validating to other people.

Record the statements you hear and the reactions you see. You'll probably notice that sometimes what is meant to be a validating statement turns out not to be, often because the person offering validation misreads the other person's feeling. For example, consider the following story:

Many months ago, eleven-year-old Brittany, who planned to be an actress, applied to a camp that offered acting classes. She was initially excited, but when the day comes to leave for camp, she has other interests and no longer wants to go. Nevertheless she packs, and her parents take her to the airport. Unfortunately, she has forgotten to pack her school ID. The airport authorities will not allow her on the plane without photo identification, so she can't make the trip. Her father, who has taken her to the airport, says, "I'm sorry about your trip. You must be disappointed." Brittany replies, "Not at all. I really didn't want to go anyway."

Brittany's father makes a reasonable statement and a comment that could be validating. It isn't, because it doesn't acknowledge the way Brittany truly feels. He makes what he intends as a validating statement in a way that shows he doesn't understand her feelings.

Practicing Nonverbal Validation

For a few hours at a time, pay attention to your friends' and family members' nonverbal language. Sometimes our nonverbal expressions are so automatic that we aren't aware of them. Watch for body language, such as crossed arms or hands on hips. Notice what people say when they run a hand through their hair or rub their temples. Perhaps people pat a foot or check their watches. Notice whether they make eye contact or look at the floor. Perhaps they giggle a lot or bite their lips. Notice your reaction to this nonverbal communication. If the nonverbal message is invalidating, the spoken statement will also be invalidating, no matter how positive the words.

Wrapping Up

Now you know what validation is and isn't. You've had an opportunity to see how well you could identify validating statements and choose them in various situations. Now that you have an idea of what validation is, we want to discuss the importance of validation in your child's growth and development. Why should you go to the trouble of learning validating parenting? We will answer that question in the next chapter.

But before we do, if you didn't complete the exercises in this chapter, please do so now. Completing the exercises on identifying validating statements and choosing them in various situations will help you understand the next chapters at a deeper level and make applying validating parenting easier. Doing all the exercises as you go along will greatly enhance your understanding of validating parenting and help you to use it successfully.

Chapter 2

The Importance
of Validation

This is the age of information. With so many ideas and suggestions concerning how to be the most effective parent, it can be confusing. Too much information, some of it contradictory, often leads people to cope with the overload by ignoring it all. This chapter addresses why learning how to be a validating parent is worth your time.

In general, validated children perform better in school, get along better with friends and others, contract fewer infectious illnesses, are more resilient in parent conflict, and grow to become more self-confident adults (Gottman 1997). They also seem better able to comfort themselves (Gottman, Fainsilber Katz, and Hooven 1997). In fact, validation seems to improve overall development. That seems like a significant payoff!

If you examine the theories of child development concerning what children need, validation is consistent with what many such theories believe children need to flourish. We believe validation contributes to the development of key characteristics that are important for children to thrive in today's world. Our children have to cope with bullying, pressure to use drugs, pressure from the media, pressure to be the best, and the many other pressures facing kids today. To resist destructive choices and not be devastated by attempts to humiliate or dominate them, children must have a solid identity and accept and value who they are. Validation helps build that sense of identity. Let's take a look at the specifics of how validating parenting can help your child's development.

How Validation Affects Identity Development

Erik Erikson, an outstanding psychological theorist who studied human development from childhood through adulthood, developed a theoretical framework for how people mature, referred to as *Erikson's eight stages of psychosocial development* (Erikson 1994). When applying validation for six- to twelve-year-olds, it helps to know more about Erikson's fourth stage, *industry versus inferiority*. In this stage the child is facing new challenges in life, and if he sees himself as successful, he can see his value. If he can't, he sees himself as inferior. If he leaves this stage with a sense of competence, then he is more prepared for the next stage: *identity versus identity diffusion*. Rather than identity development diffusion, you want your child to have ego identity, meaning that he has a solid self-image. A child with identity development diffusion is vulnerable as a teen and young adult to making decisions that don't necessarily match his value system, because he is not sure really what that is. We see validation as a means of facilitating the development of a sense of competence in stage four and then ego identity in stage five. Children in stage five of psychosocial development are generally age twelve to eighteen, depending on the child and his level of maturity. During this stage of development, the child is learning who he is. It is a critical time in development, because the child's failure to learn who he is and to build mastery during this process puts him at risk of having emotional problems as he grows older (Allen and Marotz 2003).

Stage four, ages six to twelve, is critical in preparing your child for her teen years, and parenting is so important during this time, but often parents are vulnerable because they don't know exactly what to do. Parents of children this age may try to make their child become something or someone that she is not. Remember, although parents who push their children toward a goal, such as playing a musical instrument or a specific sport, have the best of intentions, doing so can be a form of invalidation.

Consider Joe, a fifth-grader whose father played high school and college football. Joe was never an athletic child, but his father has always felt strongly that Joe should play sports. Joe has played T-ball, kid-pitch baseball, basketball, football, and golf, and he has been on the swim team every year until now—when he decided to stand up and try to be himself. Because he is neither a natural athlete nor much good at any sport he has tried, each sport he has signed up for and played has affected his self-esteem more and more negatively. He is also getting socially battered due to his inadequacies as an athlete. By nature, Joe is an artist. He wants to paint and create, but his dad doesn't approve. Joe has spent his entire life trying to be someone he is not and he endured his father's invalidation until he couldn't stand it anymore. Joe has become despondent, depressed, anorexic, and suicidal. If he cannot make his dad happy and has no idea how to make himself happy, then what can he do? This is where self-validation comes in. If Joe can learn to be okay with Joe, then that is all he needs. Letting down his father versus giving up himself is an extremely difficult choice for a child to make.

Joe's job is to discover who he is as an individual, but he is overwhelmed by pleasing his father and feels like a failure, because he believes that his true self is unacceptable. Joe has no idea how to nurture himself. A child with a healthy sense of self-validation is okay with not fitting into the mold of what someone else thinks he should be. The child who does not fit into society's molds is okay simply because he is okay, not because someone else thinks he is okay. Erikson discusses this when he addresses the ego identity development stage of his theory. Without a strong sense of his identity, an adolescent grows up to have a very complicated life. During this stage of development, children are attempting to find their own identities, not those of their mothers or fathers. It is a difficult time, one that must be successfully navigated as kids start to struggle with social interactions and grapple with moral issues. This is when Joe decides he is done with not being Joe! He must find his own identity and get validation from within, which is what he needs most to successfully navigate his life. Joe's father also has to accept his son as he is, which is not always easy for parents. People often want things for their kids that their kids themselves do not want, and you can cause suffering for your children if you impose on them your desires for their happiness rather than allow them to have their own.

Joe has the strength to assert his identity, which is separate from who his father wants him to be, and Joe's father is able to validate his son's choice. Not all children are able to accept themselves without the initial validation of a parent. Some parents are not able to validate or accept their child's true identity. Both situations can be tragic.

Our point is that validation of your child is a key component in her developing a strong identity, which is necessary for emotional health.

Mindfulness Enhances the Ability to Validate

Mindfulness means paying attention in a particular way: on purpose, in the present moment, and nonjudgmentally (Kabat-Zinn 1994). Mindfulness has been shown to be an effective tool in decreasing *emotional dysregulation*, or upset and stress (Kabat-Zinn 1990). In many situations, experiencing validation may be necessary in order to develop mindfulness (Shari Manning, pers. comm.).

To use the skill of mindfulness, you must be able to pay attention to your own experience. This awareness comes from developing a sense of your own observations, thoughts, and feelings, both concerning the external world and your internal experience. Mindfulness allows you to see what is truly real, separate from fantasies, distorted thoughts, and emotions. For example, if a child sees two friends whispering, she might believe they are talking about her or plotting ways to hurt her. When a child has the ability to be mindful, she knows that what is real is that she sees two friends talking. She is aware that she has a thought that the friends are talking about her but understands it's just a thought and not necessarily the truth. A mindful child would see the "facts" and wouldn't be swayed by what she feels or what others say. She can step back and observe her own experience, trusting what she knows to be true.

Often naturally mindful, young children are fascinated by what's happening in the moment, but because of their limited cognitive abilities, they may not understand that others see things differently than they do. Developmental psychologists say that by age eight, most children no longer engage in "magical thinking"; they know that they cannot wish for something and have it come true just because they wished for it. Many children lose their egocentric thinking, the idea that everyone sees the world as they do, and are able to understand another's viewpoint around six years of age (Sadock and Sadock 2007). The child understands that her thoughts and feelings may be different from those of others. This awareness can bring about the opportunity for greater understanding and awareness of her internal experience or a sense of shame and wrongness. Children at this age are developmentally ready to be mindful of their internal experience, and they know that their experience differs from others'. This brings about concern over whether their internal experiences are normal.

For the child, part of being mindful is being aware of his reactions, emotions, sensations, thoughts, and beliefs. A child cannot manage his emotions if he does not know what they are. He also cannot manage them if he is spending his energy avoiding experiencing them. You know what you are feeling by being mindful of your physical sensations and what event precipitated them. Being mindful of your feelings is the opposite of denying your emotional experience. Learning about your internal experience involves validation by parents or caregivers. When you learn that others accept your internal experience, you can continue to pay attention to it. If you learn that others do not accept your internal experience, then you may disregard it, distrust it, and stop paying attention to it. It's very difficult to manage your emotions and develop your own positive identity if you aren't paying attention to your internal experience. It can become difficult even to choose your favorite activity with such nonacceptance.

Adults may inadvertently, and of necessity, teach children not to be mindful. For example, a child may be fascinated by a snail slowly crawling up a wall, but consider what happens when a caregiver tells her to hurry up, that they are late and need to get somewhere. Essentially, the adult teaches the child not to be mindful. But life requires that children learn about time, deadlines, and what to pay attention to. Sometimes being mindful of time trumps being mindful of nature. Staring at a snail for hours is not effective when it's time for school, but in an effort to guide our children, we may teach them not to be mindful of critical information. When eleven-year-old Jacob is playing with sand on the beach, his father may say, "Why don't you build something?" The message is that just enjoying the sand is not okay. A mother might tell a child that he likes broccoli because he used to eat it all the time, even though he now says he doesn't like it anymore. We may ask why a child has wasted his whole day doing nothing when all the smart or popular kids are playing baseball or doing their homework. We keep children busy in classes and organized activities so that they don't have time to be bored or aware of their emotions. If they complain that they are bored, we may remind them that their grades aren't so good and they could spend the time studying. We try so hard to direct children in the right ways, but we may be inhibiting them from learning about who they are—a critical part of growing up. We can't tell them who they are, how they feel, or how they think. They need to find that out on their own.

The danger in our efforts is that we may unwittingly teach children to be unaware of their own physical sensations, such as hunger and thirst, and their own emotions, such as anger and sadness. Mindfulness is necessary to develop an individual identity, to manage emotions, and to have full awareness of internal experience. Logically, and in our experience, validation helps children develop mindfulness. When you validate a child's internal experience and behavior, you help her know that her internal experience is acceptable, and you give her permission to pay attention to it.

In turn, validation enhances a child's ability to be mindful. When he is mindful about his external and internal experience, he learns who he is, which leads to an ability to be more mindful. He can notice what he is good at and what he is not good at without scathingly judging himself. He is secure in his acceptableness. A validated child is one who is okay with how he feels, simply because he feels it. He can step back and notice his emotion, rather than merely be the emotion, and he can see that emotion as information for him to use. Because he is secure in his identity, he has confidence in his opinions and reactions and does not seek approval from others to assure himself that his internal experience is correct. He is less likely to succumb to peer pressure.

When a child is comfortable expressing her own thoughts and feelings, even if others don't share them, it can be uncomfortable for parents. Many parents of teenagers who consult us discuss how perfect their child was until she became a teenager. "Perfect" usually meant that she followed all the rules and did everything she was asked. She never disagreed, argued, or differed in opinion. The problem is that such a child is usually not developing her sense of self. When she becomes a teenager, she is at risk of doing exactly what her friends ask her to do and never disagreeing with her friends. This makes her more vulnerable to peer pressure. While it is true that some rebellion is appropriate, the invalidated child rebels outside the normal range, because she has not built the foundation of her own identity. She will likely view her parents as controlling her, because she sees her own internal experience differently than her parents do. Unfortunately because she does not know what her own internal experience is, she turns to friends and accepts what they think and feel as her own thoughts and feelings. Teaching your child to self-validate, through validating parenting, will ultimately help prepare her to ward off peer pressure and be more likely to say no and trust her internal experience, rather than what someone else thinks she should do. For example, if you have provided your child with a strong sense of validation, she is more likely than others to listen to what she knows to be right, rather than what her highly valued peer group thinks. A validated child is much less likely to get a tattoo just because everyone else is doing it if she does not really want one. She will know for herself whether that is what she wants and won't be upset if others do not agree.

How often in your life have you spent a large amount of emotional energy trying to do something that you knew was not right for you, but you did it because someone else disagreed or because you were afraid of rejection if you didn't? A child with a strong sense of self will not waste emotional energy doing this. He knows what is right for him.

Consider children with gender identity disorder and how confusing their emotional state must be. We worked with a little boy who, from the time he could walk, wore his sister's clothes and claimed that he was a girl. At first his parents thought this was cute, and they laughed and smiled at their fifteen-month-old son wearing high heels and carrying a purse. As the child grew, the parents became more and more disturbed by this behavior, which didn't seem to be going away. Over time, it started to cause strife and issues among the entire family. This little boy was seriously trying to be a girl. Interestingly, in this family, the mom got it, but the dad did not. The mom was a validating mother who even took the boy shopping for girls' clothes, which she let him wear when his dad was not home. The dad was heartbroken. He took his son hunting and boating, and even took him to strip clubs to see if he would show signs of being male. The son never did. When his mom finally sought professional help and learned about his diagnosis, it all made sense to her. He was transgendered: his internal experiences told him he was a girl. Nothing outside of him suggested that, but he felt it and did not back down. As difficult as this must be for him as he ages, his internal experiences make sense to him, which will help him as he grows up and endures all that having gender identity disorder entails. Although such issues have been covered by the news media only recently, they have been around for a very long time.

Having a secure identity is also critical for coping with bullies. If a child grows up dependent on the approval of others around her or with a pervasive sense that she is not okay, not acceptable as she is, then the bully's taunts can be devastating. The bully says aloud what the child fears or believes about herself, validating her worst fear. It's like worrying whether you might be a failure and then being told that you are. Although the bully's words may hurt the validated child, the validated child knows she is okay as a person, that the bully is not telling the truth.

Some good sources of information about mindful parenting are the book *Everyday Blessings*, by Myla and Jon Kabat-Zinn (Hyperion, 1997), and the website *Mindful Parent, Happy Child* (www.mindfulparenthappychild.com).

Validation Enhances Self-Esteem

Carl Rogers (1995) regarded personality as a triangle consisting of the real self, or the way the person actually is; the perceived self, or the way the person views herself and the way others see her; and the ideal self, or the way the person wishes to be. When all three parts fit together well, the person has *congruence*, which is a healthy mode of being. The self is an interesting and complex thing. The real self could be a funny, talented, outgoing eight-year-old. But that eight-year-old may perceive herself as a failure and disappointment, as clumsy and awkward, nothing like who she truly is. Joe's perceived self was like that. Joe's ideal self had become one that was not even close to who he was but reflected his wish to be a gifted athlete. His father perceived him as lazy, not trying hard enough, too effeminate. His father let him know that he could be an excellent athlete if he just tried harder. This caused a problem. Joe couldn't develop a healthy self-esteem, because his perceived self was nothing but negative and his ideal self didn't match who he was.

Often kids don't feel loved for who they are but feel that love is contingent on what they produce, how they do in school, or how well they played football. With validation, kids learn that they are approved of just because of who they are, not how they act or produce. For your child to find who she is, you need to allow her the freedom to express who she actually is, her real self. Joe is a great example. He felt that the only way his father would approve of him was if Joe acted in a way that did not portray his real self. He needed to be approved of as he was, not as his father wanted him to be. Validation of his real self led Joe to accept who he was.

The original definition by William James (1890) sees self-esteem as a ratio of successes compared to failures in areas of life that are important to a given individual.

James viewed self-esteem as an evaluative process; he argued that self-esteem, at its simplest, could be measured as the ratio of a person's successes to his or her pretensions. Pretensions are viewed as goals, purposes, or aims, whereas successes constitute the perception of the attainment of those goals. As people attain more of their pretensions, the ratio grows larger, and self-esteem becomes correspondingly stronger. Pretensions also add a vulnerability component to self-esteem in that these are the areas in which the individual is proposed to be most competent. If he or she comes up short in the perception of goal attainment, or in comparison with others in the same pretension arena, self-esteem suffers. A realization of shortcomings in an area that was not important to the individual, however, would not result in a devaluation of personal worth (Bernet, Ingram, and Johnson 1993, 141).

True self-esteem reflects the real value of a person, which does not depend on any specific ability compared to others but depends on her integrity as a person who fulfills her potential with regard to her unique talents and abilities. Again, it does not matter what anyone else thinks, only how the person feels about herself. If your child has a good fit among her real self, perceived self, and ideal self, then a healthy self-esteem should follow naturally, allowing further success in life. Having a high self-esteem does not mean that your child is narcissistic or arrogant or thinks she is better than others. It just means that she feels that she is fulfilling her own potential, without regard to what anyone else thinks.

Validation Helps Manage Emotions

Raising a child with validation is like giving him the gift of being able to manage his emotions so that emotions contribute to his life rather than interfere with it. Children who can cope with their feelings don't fight or deny them, mask them, or feel guilty about them. They don't seek unhealthy distractions from their internal experience, such as shopping too much, drinking too much, or losing themselves in video games.

When a child knows that her internal world is understandable, important, and acceptable to others, she doesn't have to go to extremes to get her feelings recognized. She doesn't need to shout, argue, or misbehave. Sometimes, being understood is enough. Without validation, she may not learn to acknowledge how she feels. If the child cannot learn to acknowledge how she feels, she is left with confusion and uncertainty about events that occur. She doesn't have the information that her feelings could give her. It's hard enough growing up, but when you receive feedback that your experiences and emotions do not make sense compared to everyone else's, it gets even more confusing.

Sometimes you need to take action after assuring the child that you understand his feelings, but saying that the child's feelings are understandable (and meaning it) is the first step. This doesn't mean that validating your child will always immediately stop tantrums or stop the child from making a wrong decision. It does mean that you are more likely to raise an emotionally healthy child.

We discussed previously how invalidation of feelings leads a child to believe that her feelings are unacceptable. Maybe the child learns that only anger is unacceptable or that only fear is unacceptable. The child may deny having feelings or just deny experiencing anger. Sometimes parents give the idea that feelings are unacceptable when they convey that it's important to be happy all the time. Whenever their child is sad or angry, the parents work hard to change the feeling. As does being angry or saying the child shouldn't feel a certain way, trying to change the feeling sends the message that the feeling itself is not okay. These children can become tyrants, believing that feeling bored or not getting what they want is completely unacceptable and that it's the responsibility of the parent to change their feelings.

Another issue that arises from invalidating children and leads to emotional upset is that children may learn to mask their feelings. For example, if a child learns that every time he expresses anger, his parents refuse to accept the emotion, he may learn to hide his anger from his parents, expressing it only to his friends. He may develop a lifelong pattern of not directly communicating anger to the person he is angry with, but instead communicating it to a third party. Another way of masking anger is to turn it into sadness or despair, a feeling that might elicit a more accepting response from his family. Many adults suffering from depression have this pattern. The child might turn anger into self-blame and dislike, because he feels something that is unacceptable. His self-respect would suffer, as he would automatically react to anger as if he were a bad person. He may learn to express his anger in an indirect way that does not elicit an invalidating response, such as by making hostile comments in a humorous manner. The child's parents are his guides to determining how the world works, so if they give their okay to anger expressed through humor, then the child learns to use this channel for anger. Maybe he stuffs his anger until he can't manage it any longer and then explodes.

If a child learns to mask her feelings because others don't accept her feelings, then she also begins to lose out on bonding experiences with other children. If she is sad but does not show it, she won't get support or comfort from her friends, teachers, or others who could show caring. Unfortunately, it is possible for her to interpret this as meaning that no one cares how she feels, especially when she sees her friends or other students getting comfort from the same people who don't recognize her feelings.

Children cannot get information from or manage emotions that they deny, mask, or express in indirect ways. For example, anger may mean that there is a problem to be solved. If you can't acknowledge that you are angry, it is difficult to know that there is a problem to solve, and the anger continues. Eventually the anger will result in an unhealthy behavior. If children don't learn to use the information from their feelings and manage them, they are at a significant disadvantage in making decisions about their lives. Denying and avoiding feelings takes energy. It is draining. It also often requires the help of destructive activities, such as working too much, drinking excessively, compulsively shopping, or abusing food to the point of endangering health. We create so many issues for ourselves in the name of avoiding scary feelings. Being able to validate your child's feelings will help him to learn that feelings are information and temporary. He will be more likely to be able to use the information he gets from his feelings in a wise way.

Psychologists now know that the mind is more adaptable and flexible than was previously believed for many years. We are often asked whether experiences in life can make any difference for children who are born with strong genetic tendencies toward emotional upset. Although we don't know the degree to which interpersonal experiences can overcome genetic predisposition, the research (Siegel 1999) shows that it can have an impact. Experiences and interactions with others can make a difference in a child's ability to mange her emotions.

Emotional intelligence is the degree to which someone can experience emotional empathy by paying attention to and recognizing his and others' emotions; can control his emotions and respond with appropriate (adaptive) emotions and behaviors in various life situations, especially to stress and difficult situations; and possesses good social and communication skills. Among other important consequences, emotional intelligence has proven to contribute more to workplace achievement than technical skills, cognitive ability, and standard personality traits combined (Gardner 1983). Validation facilitates emotional regulation, identity development, and the ability to form secure relationships, all of which directly contribute to emotional intelligence.

Validation Enhances Relationships

Donald Winnicott (1992) noted that everyone experiences three interlocking lives, which shape our sense of identity. The first is our internal experience of life: our emotions, sensations, thoughts, and imagination. The second life is the experiences we have through relationships with family, spouses, and friends. The third life is our experience of culture and society. The healthy personality has an anchor, or stability, in the sense of internal self. For children, the security of knowing who they are, what they want, and what they feel comes primarily through their experiences with their parents. Teachers, friends, and other adults in close relationships also contribute. All these relationships have an influence on children's views of themselves. In our opinion, children's ability to know and accept the internal self comes through validation from these highly influential people in their lives. This means that in addition to you, your child's teacher, babysitter, grandparents, Sunday school teacher, and friends' parents all have an influence on your child and how secure she feels about her identity.

Many therapists and theorists believe that the way we learn how to have relationships begins in our relationship with our caregivers. *Attachment theory* examines the ways infants bond with their primary caregivers. Three basic types of attachments have been identified: secure, avoidant, and ambivalent. A *secure attachment* leads to feelings of love, joy, and security, while significant disruptions in attachment bring about depression, anxiety, and grief (Ainsworth). The central theme of attachment theory is that mothers who are available and responsive to their infants' needs establish a sense of security. The mothers of securely attached children did not merely hold their children more than other mothers but also were more affectionate, tender, and careful. Winnicott (1992) describes them as being in tune with their children, thereby helping them understand the world. The infant knows that the caregiver is dependable, which creates a secure base for the child to then explore the world.

Validation fits the behaviors of mothers who form secure attachments with their children. Being "in tune" well describes the validation process, and the detailed descriptions of the behavior of the mothers of securely attached children strongly resemble validation. Paying attention and responding authentically to an infant's nonverbal cues is a basic form of validation.

The child with an *avoidant attachment* seeks little physical contact with the mother, is randomly angry with her, and seems unresponsive to the mother's efforts to soothe. The mother is often emotionally unavailable or rejecting, and she values the child's being independent. When the avoidant child grows older, he tends to develop the facade that he doesn't need anyone, doesn't need nurturing.

The child with an *ambivalent attachment* is clingy, needy, and chronically anxious. The mother is inconsistent, unpredictable, and not tuned in to her infant's wants. When the child grows older, she can be seen as angry and rebellious.

The child with an anxious attachment (whether avoidant or ambivalent) develops shame about who he is and negative assumptions about himself. A central feature of anxious attachment is the very act of not being attuned to. Even in infants, researchers have found what appears to be an early expression of shame when mothers do not mirror or appreciate the feelings their children express (Kaufman 1992).

The importance of attachment is not limited to the infant; it continues throughout life's developmental stages. A child's secure attachment can change in reaction to life events and changes in parenting styles.

Children who have not developed a secure attachment with their parents or caregivers may develop conduct disorders, have difficulty empathizing with others, and be oppositional or defiant with their parents. They do not have the bond with an adult that leads to a wish to please and have that adult be proud of or happy for them. The feeling that there is a lot to lose by not cooperating and listening to their parents is absent. As they grow, they may not trust others and may have difficulty disclosing intimate information to others. The attachment process is believed to continue throughout life, from infancy to death.

As a parent, you know that the attachment your child feels with you is different at three years old than at one year old, and different at twelve than at eight. Being born and growing up involves a significant separation process from parents. Being physically a part of your mother and then being held by her for most of the day is a very different experience from being six or seven, at which time you are more on your own and even going to school by yourself.

We believe that validation is a path to enhance the bond of connectedness or attachment for children. When a parent is able to respond to her infant's cues for comfort and play, which is critical for attachment, she is validating that the infant's needs are important and that she understands his emotional needs. Thus, validation enhances attachment and may be the language of attachment.

Think of how connected to someone you feel when you feel understood. That is powerful. In fact we know that healthy attachments are critical for healthy development. Validation appears to be an important factor in establishing a healthy attachment.

Validation Fosters an Internal Locus of Control

Locus of control refers to people's beliefs about what determines whether or not they get positive results in life. This characteristic is not absolute; it varies along a continuum so that people's beliefs range from very internal to very external.

People with a strong *internal locus of control* believe that the responsibility for whether or not they achieve success ultimately lies within themselves. "Internals" believe that outcomes are due to their own efforts. In contrast, "externals" believe that luck, chance, or powerful others control their life consequences. They see little effect of their own efforts on what happens to them (Rotter 1966).

Locus of control is not an either-or proposition, but a generalized expectancy that predicts people's behavior across situations. There may be some specific situations in which people who are generally externals behave like internals. That is because their experiences have shown them that they can control what happens in certain situations, even though, overall, they perceive little control over what happens to them. For example, a child who is a good student and learns easily may have a strong internal locus of control at school but a strong external locus of control at home, where her parents' reactions to her are unpredictable and don't seem to be based on her actions.

Having an internal locus of control offers advantages, in that you are more likely to work for achievements, to tolerate delays in rewards, and to plan for long-term goals. Having an external locus of control means you may be more likely to lower your goals. After failing a task, internals reevaluate future performances and lower their expectations of success, whereas externals may raise their expectations.

Individuals with an internal locus of control are better able to resist pressure from others to engage in certain activities or to change their beliefs. They are also better at tolerating ambiguous situations and have been shown to have less anxiety. People with an internal locus of control may be less prone to depression and learned helplessness than people with an external locus of control, but internals tend to be more prone to feel guilty than externals do.

People with an external locus of control are less willing to take risks, to work on self-improvement, and to complete remedial work to better themselves. Internals gain more benefits from social supports and make better mental health recovery in the long-term adjustment to physical disability. Compared to those who've learned a sense of helplessness, people with an internal locus of control do better in school, cope better with stress, and live with a greater sense of well-being. Deprived of control over their lives—an experience studied in prisoners, nursing home patients, and people living under totalitarian regimes—people suffer lower morale and poorer health (ibid.).

If a child's thoughts and feelings are validated, he knows that they matter. When he expresses his opinion, his parents listen. His efforts or lack thereof are recognized, confirming cause and effect. Validation, by its nature, encourages an internal locus of control. In fact, research by Herbert Lefcourt (1976) shows that warmth, supportiveness, and parental encouragement are related to the development of an internal locus of control. While not exactly the same, validation is accepting and supportive. It has also been said that to foster success in children, they must first feel empowered. To feel empowered, you need an internal, versus an external, locus of control. Children who regularly experience validation tend to have a better sense of self and feel more empowered individually than children who experience invalidation.

Ted has an internal locus of control. Ted's friends admire his guitar-playing skill. Some envy him and say how lucky he is to be so talented. Eleven-year-old Ted knows he is not especially talented but benefits from daily practice and the effort he puts into learning new songs. He likes being able to play but practices extra hard before parties and get-togethers with friends. Ted shows an internal locus of control.

Sam is different. Six-year-old Sam loves to play soccer so much that he plays every chance he gets, even by himself. He believes he was able to kick the winning goal in his last game because the other team got distracted and he was just in the right place at the right time. Sam shows an external locus of control.

Validation Fosters Compassion for Self and Others

Validation teaches compassion. When you validate your child, particularly when you disagree with your child's assessment of the situation, you teach her that people can have different feelings, thoughts, opinions, and beliefs, that we do not all have to be the same to respect each other and to be important. You teach your child tolerance of differences, an appreciation that she will use her entire life, whether it be in her work, her marriage, her friendships, or her view of herself. Compassion works both ways: you can have compassion for others and for yourself. Self-hate is often the result of feeling different from others around you. Self-compassion teaches that differences are not a reflection of your self-worth. For example, if you were the only Asian child in a group of friends, it would help to have learned that differences are a part of life, not a measure of the worth of human beings.

Validation also teaches a child to be compassionate toward self and others. When a child learns to validate himself, he learns to quietly assure himself that what he thinks and feels makes sense. When your child shares with you that he feels sad that he wasn't chosen for the special-select baseball team, being mindful and imagining viewing the world through his eyes will allow you to validate him and not judge his feelings as right or wrong. This is a gift. While, as a parent, you may be very well aware that his not being a part of this team is a blessing and you are secretly thrilled that he didn't make the team, your child is sad, and that is all that matters. Telling him that he will be better off not having made the team does not teach him compassion. You may be trying to help your child through the sadness, but this approach is invalidating and doesn't teach him compassion for himself and others.

Validation Fosters Perseverance

In our culture, we tend to have this mind-set that failure is a bad thing and that kids should not fail. Somehow failing becomes the same as being a failure. Yet studies of successful people show that one of the characteristics they have in common is the ability to persevere through failures (Janoff-Bulman and Brickman 1982). They are able to see failure as feedback, not as an estimate of their value as human beings; that is, failure is something they must go through in order to improve. Successful people are usually able to accept failure and learn what didn't work so they can improve. They also know that perseverance is only positive and related to success if they make good decisions about when to persevere and when to quit. Has anyone ever looked at a nine-year-old and said, "Okay, that was it, your last chance to learn math"? Probably not, but to encourage the seven-year-old to continue to ski despite the broken leg is probably not wise either.

As a parent, validating your child's feelings after a failure helps the child to move past the experience. A failure doesn't have to be sad, but if it is, then it's helpful to reassure the child that it is normal to feel that way and to struggle when learning something new. Trying to undo the feeling or change the outcome for the child is invalidating. Many parents try to fix the sadness, for instance. Fixing it is not what your child needs in this situation. Your child needs to learn that feelings are fleeting: sadness lasts only as long as the feeling sticks around, and then moves on. Conveying that emotions are like the wind, blowing through and quickly gone, is a great way to teach children about their feelings. If your child is sad that she was not chosen for the cheerleading squad, let her be sad. Her sadness will not stay for long if she is allowed to really feel it. Ask your child whether she did her best, if she had fun doing it, what she would change next time, and if the outcome was important to her. Helping your child process the experience as normal is validating and teaches her how to manage her feelings.

In *The Blessing of a Skinned Knee*, psychologist Wendy Mogel (2001) discusses how important it is for kids to fail and to learn that they can pick themselves back up and go on. She notes the importance of letting them have their small failures so that they can be prepared for the big ones. Failures are viewed as blessings because a positive outcome results. From your child's perspective, it takes practice to learn how to accept difficult emotions. It takes practice to tolerate disappointment and time to learn perseverance in adversity. Validating these experiences as normal is an important part of helping your child mature emotionally.

Validation Enhances Academic Achievement

In 1979 Harold Stevenson (1993), a professor of psychology at the University of Michigan, began a study with the object of answering a question that many Americans are curious about: why do Asian students perform better academically than American students?

Stevenson's team of researchers conducted five intensive cross-national studies analyzing student achievement in the United States, China, Taiwan, and Japan. After hundreds of hours observing students and interviewing their teachers, the researchers reached a conclusion: a key lies in what parents emphasize about their children's learning.

The difference in parenting styles is this: Asian parents strongly stress the value of effort with their children and nurture perseverance. The result is that Asian children work longer and harder than American children because of their belief that their success is based on how hard they work. American parents emphasize the final result, focusing on questions like, "What grade did you get?" "How many questions did you miss?" and "Did you win?" The effort a child puts into the process is not nearly as important to the American parent as the end product of the grade or score. Paying attention only to the end result invalidates the child's motivation and effort.

Stevenson also found that American parents place a greater emphasis on their children's innate abilities. If parents believe their child to have lower academic ability, they lower their academic expectations. Asian parents, in general, believe that any child who works hard can succeed, regardless of IQ or handicap (Stevenson 1993). Success is dependent not on ability but on how hard a child works. How validating!

Validating perseverance and effort would mean that kids learn from an early age that there's nothing to stop them from succeeding if they work hard and don't give up. Mistakes or failures would just be temporary setbacks, not excuses to quit.

One of the biggest issues we've found with validating parenting is that validation is often confused with other concepts, such as praise and encouragement. Thus many parents believe that they are validating their children when they are not. In this chapter we'll discuss in detail the differences between validation and other ways of responding to children.

Validating Is the Opposite of Shaming

In *I Thought It Was Just Me*, Brené Brown (2007) states that you cannot shame or belittle people into changing their behavior. She defines shame as that intensely painful feeling or experience of believing that you are flawed and therefore unworthy of acceptance and belonging. She points out the contradiction in our society that we support and at times encourage shaming, blaming, judgment, and rejection, but also hold acceptance and belonging as immensely important goals. Being part of a high-status group is valued and respected more than being independent. In other words, it's never been more impossible to fit in, yet fitting in has never been more important and valued.

The consequence of feeling shame is feeling disconnected from others. Shame differs from guilt. Appropriate guilt is healthy. It's about having done or said something wrong. Shame is about feeling wrong as a person. People who feel shame tend to hide and isolate themselves and believe that they deserve to be treated badly. Brown describes learning how to show compassion and empathy as the way out of shame.

June Price Tangney and Ronda L. Dearing (2002) completed an eight-year study of moral emotions (shame, guilt, and embarrassment) in almost four hundred children. A susceptibility to shame in fifth-graders strongly predicted later school suspension, drug use, and suicide attempts, whereas guilt-prone students were more likely to apply for college and be involved in community service and less likely to attempt suicide, use heroin, or drive under the influence of alcohol or drugs. The latter group also began having sex at a later age. Given that guilt is the feeling that you have done something wrong, while shame is the feeling that you *are* wrong, shame appears to be connected to destructive behavior.

Validation helps children understand that it's normal to be imperfect and make mistakes. The opposite of shaming, validation is about normalizing and understanding the child's point of view and accepting the child as a person.

Validation Enhances Happiness

Before World War I, psychologists studied emotions without focusing on mental illness. During the war, psychology shifted to focus on pathology in order to effectively treat post-traumatic stress disorder. With this shift, science progressed in uncovering the development of emotional disorders but neglected to study how people develop happiness. Positive psychology is now shifting the balance again by researching happiness, joy, and pleasure.

We know that one of the reasons happiness is important is that it builds resiliency. When you have happy times, you are better able to weather, and bounce back from, the difficult times. When you are happy, your mind broadens and is more open and accepting of new experiences. Genetically there is a set point for happiness. It turns out that a person who wins the lottery is at approximately the same level of happiness after winning the lottery as before. The person who suffers the tragedy of being paralyzed in a car accident usually experiences the same level of happiness after the accident as before the accident (Seligman 2006).

For the person with an innate ability to be happy, the genetic set point is positive, but for the person with a biological tendency to not feel positive emotions, this set point is not so desirable. Sometimes the problem is that people don't know what happiness is. They confuse it with the absence of anxiety, rage, doubt, and sadness. But happiness is something entirely different. It's the ability to receive the pleasant without grasping and the unpleasant without condemning.

There are ways to raise your happiness set point. Collecting positive memories, knowing your strengths, expressing gratitude, having fun, nurturing your relationships, savoring your experiences, thinking optimistically and acting happy, managing your time, and getting involved and finding meaning can all increase your sense of happiness. When you validate your child, it's important to validate the fun, happy, and joyful feelings as well as less-enjoyable feelings.

While access to various comforts and technologies like air conditioning, computers, airplane trips, and expensive cars may give you a buzz of pleasure, the more stable source of well-being and happiness is understanding and relating to your own mind and those of others. Compassionate relationships with yourself and others are a wellspring of happiness and health (Gilbert 2009). Validation is a key contributor to a child's ability to feel happiness and joy on a regular basis.

Wrapping Up

As we've discussed, parents sometimes wish children would never have to experience a feeling that is anything but happy and never have to know failure. As lofty and lovely as that intention may be, it's just not life. Unfortunately, life will give our children and ourselves repeated opportunities to deal with crises, and many different emotions will come as a result.

We must experience emotions to learn how to manage them. When your child feels shame, she feels shame. When she is afraid, she is afraid. Let her have her feelings and learn to manage them. Accepting your child's emotional experience helps her develop her identity, perform better in school, feel more in control over what happens in her life, and be happier. If you teach your child to trust what she feels (whether bad or good), then you are on your way to having a validated child.

Chapter 3

Applying Validating Parenting

Now that you have an understanding of the concept of validation, let's look at applying the idea to parenting and how it can help improve your children's self-acceptance and your relationship with your children and help your children learn to establish their own identities in a positive way. Marsha Linehan (1997) notes that a person can validate actions, emotions, cognitions, and physiological responses. Validation is a way of offering acceptance, which is important for a child, not only as a way to teach self-validation but also as a way to give feedback about reality. Validation and acceptance are key. If validating children's feelings means that they feel more accepted, then why would parents not want to learn more about this? First we'll discuss applying Linehan's categories of validation in different circumstances. Then we'll look at nonverbal validation and invalidation. Finally, fasten your seat belts and get ready to consider possible blocks to your success in applying validating parenting.

Validating Your Child's Physical Sensations

Understanding physical sensations and cues is an area in which parents tend to struggle to validate their children. It's hard for parents to accept that their children might understand their own bodies better than their parents do, or that parents sometimes need to help their children develop an understanding of their physical sensations. A number of children and young adults have told us that their parents tell them what they feel in their bodies. For example, parents may tell their child when they are full or when they are hungry, or when they are tired or when they aren't. A child who tells her mother that she is still hungry may get this response from the mother: "How could you still be hungry? You just ate a whole plate of pasta and cake for dessert. What's wrong with you that you still have an appetite? There's no way that I would still be hungry if I had eaten that." With these comments, the child learns to distrust her own internal experience of hunger or satiety. The child also may feel shame that her appetite differs from her mother's.

Consider another example. On a road trip, even though it was 98 degrees outside, Lucy consistently complained to her parents that she was cold, and even asked them to turn on the heat. Her siblings were getting annoyed with her, and everyone in the car told her she was crazy for being cold. She eventually gave up and shivered all the way through Texas as the family headed to Colorado for the summer. It was not until they stopped for the night that Lucy's mother finally attended to her complaints. It turned out that she had a fever of 104 degrees and was extremely ill with the flu. She was cold because she had a high fever. While her physical sensations had made no sense to anyone else, they made sense to her.

Learning to ignore the body's cues can also be damaging to mental health. Ignoring satiation and hunger cues is partly why eating disorders develop. Mothers invalidate their children by telling them how much, what, and when they should eat. They encourage their daughters to join the "clean plate" club, even if the children are very clear that they are no longer hungry. The parent's goal is not to invalidate body sensations, of course, but unfortunately that can be the outcome.

Sometimes children complain of stomachaches when they are afraid or don't want to do something, which can create a difficult situation. Allowing children to avoid something because of a physical ailment that isn't related to a physical illness encourages the reoccurrence of that behavior. Telling a child he isn't sick is risky, because you don't know for sure and you might invalidate him. If you have reason to think he is avoiding something but there's no physical evidence, validate that he doesn't feel well. Try not to make assumptions, and recognize that there are many different ways people can feel bad. Perhaps discuss with your child how sometimes people don't feel well when they are worried or scared about something. Mention that your child perhaps is not feeling well because of anxiousness or nervousness. Note that it's normal to want to stay home when you're afraid of something. Even if your child continues to deny that this is the reason, you have provided important information. He might really be sick.

Emotions are tied to physical sensations as well. If Audrey complains that her stomach feels "jumpy," you could take it as an opportunity to help her connect her physical sensations with her emotions by asking if she is nervous or worried about something. Children are not born knowing how to label emotions or recognize them. They are born knowing how they feel inside.

Validating Your Child's Emotional Experience

Every day, your child has emotional experiences that help prepare her for adulthood. While Caroline's being upset about not getting the outfit she wanted or about a friend's bowing out of coming over to play may not seem significant, and is an interruption you don't need, helping her practice handling her emotions is important. Knowing how to handle sadness and other emotions is a critical skill. Helping your child accept and know her own feelings helps her cope with them. If you think you know the reason for her feelings, mentioning the cause helps her connect her upset to the event. For example, when your child is in tears because she doesn't want her friend to leave, you would validate her feelings if you said, "I know it's hard to say goodbye. You want her to stay," or, "Wow, you must have had a great time for it to be so hard to say good-bye to your friend." At the same time, if she responds that your guess is wrong, be ready to listen to her.

It's important that you communicate to your children in this way. But is that what most of us do? No way. Most often, we respond that the child shouldn't feel as she does: "She'll be back. Come on, now, I let her stay an extra half hour," or maybe "If you act like this, I'll never let her come over to play again." Sound familiar?

Parents don't want to encourage their children to be ungrateful. When the child expresses sadness that a friend has left, it can sound pretty selfish. Often the parent's thoughts are *Wow, what a brat*. It's hard to validate when you don't agree, particularly when the child's feelings seem unreasonable. Remember, validation means only that you recognize how the child feels; it doesn't mean you necessarily agree.

Seven-year-old Joshua wants a bike for his birthday. His neighborhood friends ride their bikes together after school, and Joshua feels left out. He works hard in school and listens to his parents' guidance. He tells his parents he wants a black one, but it doesn't really matter. His parents warn him that they might not be able to afford a bike this year. Joshua wants the bike so badly he can't listen. He marks the days off the calendar, counting down to his special day. For his birthday, Joshua's parents give him a party with his friends and his favorite cake. His parents give him several presents, but he doesn't get a bike. Joshua starts crying and goes to his room. His mother understands and validates his experience, saying, "I know you had your heart set on a bike. And I know that right now, having a bike is the most important thing in the world to you. I'm sorry you are disappointed and upset." Joshua continues to cry but feels understood and that his feelings are accepted. His mother doesn't call him selfish or spoiled or shame him for his feelings. She validates his experience and realizes that her knowing and acknowledging that a bike could be so important to him could help ease his feelings and help him accept the situation. She also knows she isn't a bad parent for being unable to give him something he wants. Sometimes parents believe that if they accept the validity of their child's feelings, then they are wrong for not changing the situation. That is not the case. You cannot always make your children happy or fix what makes them sad, but you can help them learn how to manage such feelings through the power of validation.

Validating Specific Emotions

Validating emotions can be challenging. We all much prefer that our children be happy, and sometimes it seems to us that they wallow in their sadness. Sometimes, too, their emotions can bring us down, and we really don't want that, especially if there doesn't seem to be a good reason for their reactions. At other times, our children's expressions of intense emotion anger us. Then again, when they are happy about a success, we worry that they may become too arrogant. Parenting is difficult yet rewarding, and learning to validate these emotions may help in raising a more emotionally healthy child.

ANGER

Seven-year-old Marissa has been troubled by anger all day. She is bored, didn't like breakfast, and wants to go to a friend's house. You say no. Her younger brother is playing quietly, and she knocks over his tower of blocks. He cries, and she calls him a name. Marissa calls him a baby and takes his stuffed animal. You stop her. Validating her feelings will not come naturally in this situation. "I understand that you feel angry with your brother" will be difficult to say. Her behavior is unacceptable, and all you want to do is tell her what's what: "You are being a brat," or "Don't you dare hit your brother." But saying these words will probably increase Marissa's anger, upsetting her even more. Marissa screams, "I hate you!" Perhaps she even tries to hit you. The validating parent accepts the anger but not the behavior, "I understand that you are angry, but it's not okay to hit or to hurt other people." This statement validates her feelings, gives her a label for how she feels, and sets limits on her behavior.

Try not to shame the child for feeling angry. Instead take a moment to guess why Marissa is having a difficult day and offer her an idea of what might be making her angry. You could ask questions to help Marissa discuss what upset her.

Validating and listening may be exactly what you would do for a good friend who is angry. You are doing the same for your children, but they may need help connecting their anger with the triggering event. Helping your child to connect with what he is actually feeling and what triggered the feeling increases his emotional skills.

One easy way to help your child connect feelings with events is to guess. If you know approximately when the feeling started, you can ask questions about what happened around that time. When you hear something that would have triggered that feeling in you, you can guess that this event likely is the reason your child feels this way. Remember, it's just a guess. You could be wrong. In fact, you probably are wrong. But it's a good place to start.

Adults feel comforted when someone really listens to them, and children are no different. When adults recognize their feelings and show that they care by expressing interest, elaborating, or guessing about additional details, children feel acknowledged and valued. Many times, the anger dissipates when someone listens.

FEAR

Young children do not yet have a good understanding of what is real and what isn't. A young child may believe there's a monster in his room at night. That monster is real to him. When your child screams for help at night and says there's something in his room, his fear is real. To help him feel safe, you might reassure him by saying that there are no monsters and that he is safe because you are there with him and won't let anything happen to him. Saying that there's nothing to be afraid of invalidates the child. He knows he is afraid, and someone much wiser, whom he trusts and depends on, is telling him he shouldn't feel the way he does. Because he knows he is afraid, telling him there's nothing to be afraid of doesn't help him. Yet you must tell the truth. Remember, validation is never about lying.

Telling a child that he is safe because his parents are with him is not enough. That gives the child the idea that he can be safe only when he is with his parents, and it doesn't help him develop skills to manage his own feelings. So what do you say? Some situations, like this one, can seem tricky. Remember to validate the feeling or thought: "It would be scary to me too, if I believed monsters were in my room," or "I get scared sometimes too. We all do."

What about when the fear is based on possibilities that are real? A child might be scared that her mother, who is very ill and must go through surgery, will die. Or perhaps she is scared when the winds of a powerful storm are beating at the door. Validating your child's feelings is still helpful: "Yes, the weather can be scary. Sometimes it scares me too," or "I'm scared about this surgery too. It's normal to be scared."

When they are actually afraid, kids sometimes believe they need to throw up, due to unease in the pit of the stomach. Helping them to see what's causing the stomach discomfort frees them from expressing their emotions through body aches and pains. Using validation will help you figure out what's really going on.

WORRY

Some children are worriers. Parents don't want their children to worry and repeatedly tell them to stop. We all know how well that works, but we still do it. Most of the time, it's easy to see why someone else shouldn't worry, especially children. We may say something like, "What have you got to worry about?" We may even ask ourselves that question, but it doesn't stop the worry. Worry, just like fear, can happen for productive and unproductive reasons (Leahy 2005). People tend to worry about the things they are afraid of. If you are afraid of storms, then you will probably worry when a storm is in the forecast. Worry can be helpful when it motivates you to prepare for the storm. That is productive worry. If you are worried about your friend's health when there's nothing wrong with your friend and no action to take, then this is unproductive worry. Unfortunately, sometimes people worry about what they are afraid of but do not take any action, creating a constant state of uneasiness.

Validation will probably not stop a child from worrying. As much as you want your child to stop worrying, that probably won't be the outcome. Nevertheless, validation remains important. "Being worried about storms doesn't feel good, does it!" is one validating response when there's no imminent danger from a storm. "Storms can be scary. What is it that worries you about this one?" If you and your child have been through a similar upsetting event, you could say, "I remember last year's storm too. That was a very scary experience. It makes sense that you are scared." After you validate the feeling, you can give information about the different levels of storms: some are hurricanes, and some are weaker.

Understanding the difference between productive and unproductive worry can be helpful. For a better understanding of the purpose of worry and how to cope with it, you might wish to read *The Worry Cure: Seven Steps to Stop Worry from Stopping You*, by Robert Leahy. Although he doesn't address worry in children, you can use the information to help your children.

JEALOUSY AND ENVY

Jealousy usually refers to the fear of losing something or someone by substitution. Envy means bearing a grudge toward someone for what he has or enjoys. In a milder form, envy means, absent of ill will, wanting something that someone else enjoys. Parents often have to deal with both jealousy and envy. Jealousy can occur between children who fear losing the affection of their parents to siblings. Envy may be evident when your child wants to play ball, sing, or have clothes like one of her friends. The simple part is that validation does not change. When your child expresses envy or jealousy, validate the feeling. Listen carefully to the reasons your child feels the way she does. Maybe a sibling has been getting more attention lately.

HAPPINESS, JOY, AND FUN

Strangely enough, many adults aren't comfortable with happiness. Happy people are sometimes considered naive, fake, or Pollyannaish, or they're regarded as people who don't really understand how hard life is. Sometimes people fear the loss of happiness, so they don't want to feel happiness at all. Helping your children understand that happiness is not a permanent state can be helpful to them. Validate the importance of laughter, having fun, and happiness. Modeling happiness is a way of showing the normalcy of feeling that emotion. Validation can be used with positive emotions as well as more difficult feelings.

Feelings about Emotions

Besides the reasons already discussed, validating less-pleasant feelings is important because sometimes children feel ashamed or afraid of unpleasant emotions. They sometimes don't understand that these emotions are normal. If a child reacts to his anger by being ashamed of it, then he has increased his emotional upset. If a child is afraid of feeling sad, then when he feels sad, he will also feel afraid, which makes coping with the emotion that much more difficult. Validating children's unpleasant emotions helps them accept their feelings as normal and prevents their becoming more upset from having negative feelings about their emotions. While children may have negative reactions to pleasant emotions, such as fearing happiness, the more typical experience is to have unpleasant beliefs about the feelings that are typically less acceptable to others. A child who feels guilty or sad about any emotion will be less likely to talk with you about it. Part of being a validating parent is acting as a safe container in which your child can truly express himself.

Validating Your Child's Behavior

You can validate many aspects of your child's behavior, but we will discuss just a few here. The idea is to allow independence, interests, and imperfection while recognizing and accepting your child's weaknesses and strengths.

Validating Independence

Not doing for your children what they can do for themselves validates their independence. For example, imagine that you are tired after a long day of work and parenting. Your nine-year-old daughter ate very little at dinner because she wanted to go back to playing with her friends. Now that the dinner dishes are washed and the food is put away, she tells you she is hungry. Your emotions may control how you respond. You may tell her she cannot be hungry and that she must go to bed. Or you might prepare her food, resenting every minute, and tell her that this had better not happen again. Allowing independence and competency would be to validate her hunger but tell her that if she is still hungry, she can prepare her own snack and clean up afterward.

If your child's attire is a constant battle for you, try validating her independence by letting her choose her own clothes. She may wear the same dress every day for two weeks. She may pair a pink tutu with a green football jersey that you think looks ridiculous. Perhaps worse, perhaps you imagine that other parents see her outfits and think you're a hideous, inattentive parent. Remember, try not to let your emotions control how you behave. Allowing your child independence with how she dresses will defuse any battle you two may have had over clothes. She gets the opportunity to be independent in an acceptable way. She will likely figure out what outfits work and don't work without your taking over.

Validating Interests

Chloe, aged seven, wanted to take apart every computer in the house to investigate how it was made and to see if she could rebuild it after dismantling it. Her mom could not understand this behavior from her young daughter and kept pushing Chloe to play with dolls instead of electronics, but Chloe wasn't interested. Her mother knew that most of Chloe's friends played with dolls, and she wanted her daughter to be part of the group. To Chloe's detriment, her mother often pushed her into activities the mother wanted her to do. Her mother tried to shame Chloe out of her interest in electronics and even forbade her from pursuing it. If her mother did this in other situations, the experience could lead Chloe to doubt her preferences in general or to see her choices as wrong. She could constantly invalidate herself, creating indecision, self-doubt, and misery. This is exactly the opposite of what you want as a parent. You want your child to know her own preferences and make choices based on her own beliefs, to feel okay simply because she knows she is okay, not because anyone else tells her she is.

Another possible outcome is that Chloe will reject all of her mother's suggestions, because her mother obviously doesn't get that Chloe wants to be the next Steve Jobs. How can her mother understand anything about her if she doesn't understand that?

Chloe's mother means well. She sees her daughter's engaging in play with kids her age as a step to giving her the best social chances in life. That may be a reality. A girl taking apart and rebuilding electronics in the second grade may not be as popular as the girls who play with dolls, but it's also true that Chloe has an interest in computers and that's part of who she is. You don't want to tell her that her interests are wrong, because that also sends the message that Chloe is wrong as a person.

Validating Weaknesses and Strengths

One of the traits of happy people is that they know their strengths and use them. You can help by validating your children's strengths. This is not about attempting to create strength in a certain area by telling children they are good at golf or art, hoping they will become the next Arnold Palmer or

Vincent van Gogh. It's about noticing what your child does well and recognizing that. Your child's strengths could be personality traits, such as being kind to others, being good at making friends, or being a good sport at games.

More difficult perhaps is validating your child's weaknesses. Nine-year-old Eric comes home crying because he was the last one chosen for basketball. He says, "I'm horrible at basketball." It's true that he's not good at basketball. The first thing to validate is how he feels about not being chosen, a painful experience most of us have had at some point. The second thing to validate is that he might not be the best at basketball; but did he have fun? Only then do you consider solving the problem, such as helping him practice his skills if he wants. He may not want to work at getting better, and that would be okay too. Kids cannot be the best at everything. Take a look at your own parenting style. Are you setting up the expectation that your kids can't have weaknesses? If so, remember that even Superman has his kryptonite.

Accepting weaknesses helps eliminate the shame we tend to feel about them. Paul Gilbert (2009) notes a difference between shame and disappointment, explaining that shame is not so much about our not meeting our own standards, but more about moving closer to being undesirable in our own eyes and those of others. The reason people don't want to move closer to that undesirable self is that it brings the threat of rejection, humiliation, and non-acceptance. Parents want to help their children believe *I'm not as good a player as I'd like to be* instead of *I'm bad*. Separating the behavior from the person changes the threat and helps keep the experience from being a shameful one.

ACCEPTING IMPERFECTION

If your child thinks that her stomach is fat when you absolutely know it's not, allow her to think what she thinks. Because you know that she looks wonderful, it does not make sense to you, but it does to her. Validating her thoughts will lessen their intensity. If she thinks she is imperfect, no amount of your conveying the opposite will help. Some parents might respond to a daughter, "You don't have a fat stomach, but if you'd like to change something, you could stop all that nighttime cookie eating." In suggesting that she do something about it, you are essentially agreeing with your daughter's feeling that she is fat, which is not validating. Remember that validating your child's thoughts does not mean agreeing. There's a big difference between "I know you believe your stomach is fat. I don't agree, but I know you think that" and "Stop being ridiculous" or "You could lose a few pounds." The latter responses suggest that she should change herself based on her thoughts, which is what this book is trying to warn against. The goal is to help your child avoid basing her thoughts and sense of reality on something that has no basis in reality.

Children can "feel" as if they have no friends, don't fit in, or any of a number of different negative situations. This is basing thoughts on feelings. Arguing with your child probably won't change her interpretation of reality, because it's not based on logic. Validate her perception or thought as her perception or thought, and let her know that you do not see things the same way.

Validating Your Child's Thinking

Children have a lot to learn in so many areas: how to make choices, what's normal, how their thoughts may be the same or different from others', and how to trust their intuition. They need to learn how to test their thinking for accuracy. Parents have opportunities to help children in these areas in ways they may not realize.

Validating Choices

If an eleven-year-old had to choose between having a fully funded retirement plan and a new computer, most would choose the computer. Perspectives are different when you are eleven than when you are thirty.

When your preteen daughter comes downstairs dressed for school in torn jeans and chains, you may want to say, "I'm not letting you out of this house in that ridiculous attire. Go back upstairs right now and put on something decent." A more validating comment might be "I get it that you like that style and that you think that outfit is great, but it's not appropriate for school." You still require her to change clothes because of your own guidelines or the school's, but you do so while validating her choices. Notice that even if the school allows the outfit, you don't have to agree with that choice.

Here's another example. Your six-year-old son has a friend over to play. Your son chooses a toy, and his friend takes a different one. Your son becomes angry and cries that his friend took the toy he wanted. Your first thought might be to lecture him about not being selfish. As a parent you believe that learning to share is an important part of growing up. But that's not the point in this moment. Your little boy is angry. A validating response would be, "It's really hard to share your toys. Right now, you feel as if you must have the toy he chose." First, you validate his feelings, and then you give the lesson about sharing. Logic doesn't work to calm emotion. Validation does.

Validating Normalcy

Feelings are not logical. They are also different for everyone and cannot be compared to how nine out of ten people would feel in the same situation. Sometimes feelings and thoughts are not pretty, but they are not to be judged as good or bad. They just are. Validation is recognizing that there is an internal experience that's not necessarily the same as someone else's and may not even match reality in the external world.

Validation is also a way of letting your child know that he is normal. Most people have doubts that their internal experiences are normal, so they hide what they think and feel. Invalidating a child's emotions confirms his worst fears that his thoughts and feelings differ from those of others. This in turn makes him think that he isn't acceptable.

Imagine being a child whose beauty her mom and dad consistently praise, but who is teased at school about having large ears. What if you did not feel beautiful, yet people older and wiser than you said you were? Believe it or not, it's invalidating. That little girl may say to herself *I feel ugly, but they think I'm pretty, and they must know more.* As strange it sounds, this sets the stage for invalidating that little girl's internal experiences. She may say to her mom, "I don't think I'm beautiful." The mother, uncomfortable with her daughter having these thoughts, of course, argues and teaches the girl to distrust her own internal experiences. While seemingly innocuous, if pervasive this response is extremely harmful.

What do you say? How can you validate that your child doesn't feel pretty? Find out what's bothering her. In this case, she's being teased about her large ears. Just tell the truth: "You believe you have large ears, and that makes you think you are not beautiful." She will agree or not. If she doesn't agree, then keep trying until you understand what she's trying to say. Does she believe her ears make her unattractive or ugly, or simply not beautiful? The specifics are important. Once she agrees, validate her feeling. "If I believed I had large ears and that made me feel ugly, I'd be upset too, especially if other people teased me about it. That's really hard."

If this sounds harsh to you, consider the alternative. Your saying that your child is pretty and that the kids at school don't know what they are talking about doesn't change her experience. What it may do is make her feel that you don't understand her. She then keeps her feelings to herself and has to deal with the situation alone. Validation keeps the doors open to communication.

For many parents, the problem is letting their children struggle with issues that upset them. Supporting children as they deal with problems teaches resiliency and coping skills. Using validation, you confirm to the child that what he feels is legitimate and that he knows his own feelings better than anyone else does.

Sometimes, when it's true, you'll confirm that what the child feels fits the situation and is logical and that others would feel the same way. When a child is sad that a beloved grandparent had to cancel a visit, that's a situation most people would feel sad about. At other times children's feelings may be unique to them. Because John loves cats so much, it's understandable that he would be worried that the cat didn't get to come on the family vacation.

Validating Children's Reactions to Others

Ten-year-old Angela complained to her mother that she didn't want to go visit Uncle James: "I hate Uncle James. He's mean." Children don't always like the same people their parents like, whether they are friends their own age or family members. Validate your child's feelings and then ask why she doesn't like the person. Maybe there's something you need to know. Adults don't always treat children the same way they treat other adults. Even if Angela doesn't have a good reason, she gets to choose whom she likes and doesn't like. Family relationships may require respect and attention, but liking or loving someone cannot be required.

Sometimes parents throw their children's feelings under the bus to save face for themselves. We tell children to keep quiet so that they don't cause a stink or create problems with family or neighbors. Eleven-year-old Claire babysat regularly for the neighbor's grandchildren. One day the grandfather hit Claire in anger. She told her mother, who said she was sure he wouldn't do it again and suggested that Claire say nothing because the man was a nice neighbor. Claire never went back but was given no support for setting boundaries.

Wrapping Up

This chapter covered the basic ways to apply validation in parenting. You can validate thoughts, actions, physical sensations, and emotions. We listed some specific applications that we see as important and gave some examples. In addition, we discussed the role of validation in discipline, nonverbal validation, and blocks to success in applying validation to parenting.

Validation is not about stopping any emotional state from happening. Sometimes that's the result and sometimes not. Whether or not validation diminishes the emotion, validating is still important. Sometimes you will see positive results from validating difficult emotions, such as anger, jealousy, fear, and worry, and sometimes you won't. Because you don't see positive results does not mean that your efforts won't result in an emotionally healthy child. Sometimes the effectiveness of validation is not evident for many years, and often the change is not visible but internal.

Chapter 4

Why Parents Invalidate

It's often difficult for parents to validate their children; in fact, it's one of the hardest things for parents to practice, perhaps because it's too simple and therefore easy to overlook. It's difficult not only for parents but also for everyone. As an example, think about dieting. Everyone knows the "magic" to losing weight: eat less, exercise more. It's simple to understand yet difficult to do. In the United States, diet products and services are a major industry. It seems as if people spend a lot of time and money on finding easier ways to do things. There's no easy way to be a validating parent.

The only time validation is easy to apply is when you actually agree with what your child feels and thinks. But if your child says something you believe is unfair or ridiculous, how can you just stand by without telling your child how wrong he is? This may seem inconsistent, as if you were going against your natural urges as a parent. After all, isn't it part of your job to teach your child right from wrong? Remember Carter from the first chapter? In his mother's eyes, he was actually acting appallingly ungrateful and pathetic. She felt that he was the most ungrateful child on the planet and had the urge to punish him for his feelings. As a mom, shouldn't she have told Carter how ungrateful he was acting? The answer is yes and no. Carter's mom had a responsibility to allow him to have his feelings. She smelled like the sardines used to help him feed the seals, and she was hot, tired, and exasperated, but so was he. He needed to feel his feelings. His mother did not have to agree or allow his feelings to change her behavior, but she needed to allow him to feel. This is one of the main reasons validation is so hard to apply. It feels unnatural to allow your child to have such a fit over a lollipop.

Let's look at another area in which validation is difficult. Have you ever wondered how you ended up in your family? You are probably very different from your parents, but maybe you have siblings who are just like your parents. Having the same DNA or genetic makeup doesn't mean you'll have the same values. Now think about your own children. Think about how different each one of them is. They probably have different values than you do and perhaps than their siblings do. Now imagine how hard it is to validate a child when his values and interests differ from yours. You may strongly value eating organic foods and taking care of the environment. Suppose your child values trendy new gadgets and high-tech toys and has no concern for the environment. He doesn't even want to recycle. Parents don't have to violate their own values, but they can't expect their child to conform to them. This is difficult. Here's an example: Suppose you are a parent who finds immense pleasure in reading. It's your entertainment, your peace, and your encouragement. But your son doesn't want to sit still and read, and he derives no pleasure from reading. He is skilled in math and science and is the fastest runner on the block. He just doesn't like to read. Can you change him? Probably not. Despite having a strong urge to get your children to conform to your values, doing that would risk invalidating their values. We (the authors) can remember how that felt when we were children, and we bet you can too. Many such situations challenge parents who are practicing validation.

We haven't forgotten about you. Parents need validation too. When parents lose their temper or say things they know are invalidating, most are upset with themselves. Very few parents invalidate out of disregard for or hatred of their children. Read on to learn more.

Parents Misinterpret What It Means to Be Close

When parenting a baby, you are required to learn the baby's cues. The parent responds to the baby's needs based on their close experiences day to day, on knowing what the baby usually wants when she makes certain sounds or movements. This closeness is difficult to give up. You want to be there to meet your child's every need. Some parents believe they know their children better than the children know themselves. After all, the parents have an adult perspective and have observed their children's patterns over the years. Unfortunately, an "I know you better than you know you" attitude inhibits the child from developing healthy independence. Part of maturing is for the child to know herself and be able to express her own needs and desires to others. Closeness between parent and child is based on allowing the child to develop this independence and a sense of self. The parent must adjust to the child's changing needs. If the parent is not willing to allow this growth, problems in the child's development can occur. Take twelve-year-old Molly, who is in counseling for depression and anxiety. When Molly describes her parents, she refers to them as "Mommy and Daddy." When her therapist asks her why she calls them Mommy and Daddy, Molly replies that her parents have expressed to her many times that they do not want her to grow up and that by being called "Mommy" and "Daddy," they still feel that she needs them. This seems insignificant, but it's not. Molly's main reason for depression and anxiety stems from her parents' inability to let her go. She desperately wants to grow up but is deathly afraid of what that would do to her parents. Her parents need to let her grow up and separate for Molly to become the person she is meant to be. They do not know her better than she knows herself anymore. She is growing up, and this scares her parents.

Parents Don't See the World from the Child's Point of View

Parents get incredibly upset and confused when their children are sad for seemingly no good reason. It's upsetting enough to see your children be sad when you believe they actually have a good reason to feel that way, but when you believe they don't, it's just downright annoying. Because you love them, you want your children to be happy. Most of the time, you willingly sacrifice for their happiness. When your child expresses sadness over not getting to go to the zoo when he was just there last week or even yesterday, your innate tendency as a parent is to invalidate, telling the child he has nothing to be sad about because he was recently at the zoo. You also might throw in all the things for which your child should be grateful. While that may be true from your point of view, it clearly isn't what the child is expressing.

You may *know* that your child has many reasons to be happy and few reasons to be sad, but your perceptions come from having a different life than your child does. What's important to your child is different from what was important to you at the same age. In fact what is important to your child at sixteen will be different from what was important to you at sixteen. Take Brian, for instance, whose father grew up in Germany during World War II. Brian's father's life was very different from his own. As a little boy, his father endured scarcity and worry about where his next meal would come from. Being Jewish, Brian's father's family lived in fear of the Nazi regime. Thankfully, they emigrated successfully and built a new life in the United States without the trials and tribulations they had experienced in Germany. Imagine how different Brian's concerns as a youth growing up in the United States are from his father's concerns when he was growing up in Nazi Germany. Often Brian's father tries to compare Brian's concerns to his as a young boy, which just doesn't work. They are from two different worlds, and Brian is more concerned about not having the best MP3 player than his physical safety, which his father often frowns on. His father feels that because Brian is safe from tyranny and war, and does not live in fear of imprisonment, he should be content. It doesn't work that way. Brian needs validation for his concerns and fears as much as his dad did at his age, even though their experiences have been completely different. Giving your children your logic, wisdom, and experience is important. Telling your child his feelings are not valid or that he is spoiled or ungrateful doesn't work.

Children's worries often don't make sense to parents. Parents often don't see things from their children's viewpoint. When your daughter expresses fear that you will die in a car accident, you tuck her in and respond that there's no reason to worry about that. Or if your son says he is scared that your family won't have enough to eat someday, you may joke that you have way too much to eat because everyone in the family needs to lose about ten pounds. As ridiculous as these fears are to you, they are real to your children. If you think back to when you were a child, you probably had many of these same feelings and behaviors, but as an adult, you have a different perspective. As adults, we are better able to manage our emotions (fear and disappointment, especially), and need to teach and shape our children to learn this as well. Our ability did not magically appear; we learned it, probably through being validated by others.

Think about the first time a relationship broke your heart. Remember how sad you were, how you believed you would never be happy again and were ready to lie down on the road and let a truck run over you? Now think back to how your parents responded. They may have said, "Aw, that one was a loser anyway," "You are too young to know what love is," "You are better off without that person," or "Someone else will come around who is better." Think about the invalidating messages in those statements, which were intended to make you feel better. Did they succeed? Probably not. You probably felt as if no one understood how horribly you were hurting. You may have felt that you could never love anyone again or that you didn't know what real love was. You needed to grieve, be sad, and learn that life moves on despite heartbreak. If someone had said to you, "I'm so sorry you are upset," that probably would have felt very soothing and helped you to cope better with your feelings. Think about when you were a teen. Whom did you choose to talk with about upset feelings? How did that person respond to you? The person you liked to talk with was quite probably someone who took your feelings seriously and didn't judge or berate you or tell you how you should feel.

Parents Don't Want Their Children to Be Selfish

Sometimes children are sad for apparently selfish reasons. When you've done so much for your child, that hint of selfishness can be maddening. It may seem that by being sad, the child is invalidating all the parent has done for her. No parent would like that. Parents also don't want their child to grow up feeling entitled. In the example of seven-year-old Carter wanting the lollipop, the mother does not agree with her son. She thinks it's ridiculous that he is so upset. The boy is being uncharacteristically demanding, and his mother wants to tell him to get a life, deal with it, and get over it. While that may seem a good option to build character, it doesn't work. It would only teach the boy to distrust his internal experiences, which could set him up for a lifetime of confusion. As much as Carter's mother wants her son to be grateful for the fun day she has provided him with, she also knows that what he feels makes sense and is logical to him. Remember that just because you allow your child to feel his feelings doesn't mean that you agree or allow him to act on them.

Parents Misunderstand Validation

In an earlier chapter, we noted that many parents think validating parenting is permissive parenting. In fact, validation is not about your disciplinary style at all. Shaming or otherwise invalidating your child doesn't work to get her to change. In fact it probably would backfire.

Validating does not mean that children do not have to do things they don't want to do, just as it doesn't mean that you agree with what you are validating. Validating does not mean allowing your children to hit, yell, or destroy property to express their feelings. Validating parenting does not mean that your children get away with murder.

Feelings are separate from actions. Validating anger does not mean that there is no consequence for acting out of anger, such as by yelling or throwing something. In fact validating a child's feelings without accepting his actions teaches him to not allow his feelings to control him and to not act impulsively. To teach a boy that he is allowed to be angry is extremely healthy. To teach him to not respond in anger is even better. It will be helpful for you to remember that validating the feeling does not mean accepting the action.

For example, Hamilton, aged eleven, loves to ski. His family took him to Colorado last spring break. In his parents' opinion, Hamilton is not a safe skier. He speeds through treed areas and goes over jumps without much skill. His parents decide that he must wear a helmet if he wants to ski, but he doesn't want to wear a helmet. He feels that he is being babied and says he won't ski if he has to wear a helmet.

His parents respond, "We understand that you feel like you're being babied, but you still have to wear the helmet. If you choose not to ski, that's your decision." Hamilton chose to wear the helmet and ski. His parents would have been just fine if he had chosen to stay in the hotel. They don't allow his anger to control how they parent him, yet they validate his frustration.

Parents Want to Fix What Is Wrong

Parents want to fix their children's problems so they can be happy. Sometimes parents "fix" sadness or other emotions by telling the child that what she feels doesn't make sense, sometimes even doing so in a judgmental way. Statements like "I can't believe you're this upset about that," and "You are such a whiny baby," are examples. Parents also try to fix emotions by buying children presents to make the feeling go away or by taking them for treats to mitigate their sadness. This sends a message that happiness is the only feeling that's okay. By using this tactic, we teach our children that sadness is a horrible thing, a thing to avoid discussing and to get rid of fast. This sounds like a setup for a feel-good lifestyle, doesn't it? Parents use presents, ice cream, and skating in much the same way that people use excessive shopping, drugs, alcohol, and other numbing activities. Although you may be doing this to stop your child's difficult feeling, unfortunately this teaches children to numb their feelings, which, down the road, can lead to avoidant behaviors, such as drug abuse or eating disorders; depression or anxiety; obsessive-compulsive disorder; and other emotional disorders.

What would you do if your child came home from school complaining of being bullied? That's what Chase does. His parents are especially upset that he is being bullied and that it is a smaller classmate bullying him. He comes home daily feeling sad and mad, venting about the situation. His parents have already changed his school twice for reasons related to interpersonal conflicts with schoolmates. Changing schools again may seem like the way to solve the problem, but the school is not the problem. As his parent, you want to tell him to stand up for himself, to buck up, fight his battle. It's painful that he's letting a smaller child push him around. You want to fix it but can't. Using validating parenting would give Chase a safe space to allow you to help him. Just being present can be validating. It might mean doing nothing at all, or it might mean getting Chase some help with his interpersonal skills. Validation will help you know what to do.

Parents Don't Want Their Children to Talk Back

Sometimes when children say that a parent hurts their feelings or doesn't listen to or understand them, parents may feel defensive and see the child as being disrespectful and talking back. "Don't tell me I don't understand. The problem is I understand all too well," might be a parent's response. If you stop, take a breath, and think about it, maybe the child doesn't grasp that you understand how important this is to her or that you know she thinks what she wants will make her happy forever but you are still saying no.

While you may listen and understand exactly what the child is saying, perhaps the child doesn't see that. Or maybe the child is correct in thinking that you aren't listening. It's important for a child to be able to say that he doesn't feel heard or that you hurt his feelings. And it's important as well for you to be able to say to your child that it seems that he isn't listening or that he hurt your feelings. You need to give information about feelings in a respectful way, but *having* feelings of being unheard is not disrespectful.

Sometimes it might seem easier to invalidate your child, to shut her down. If your child complains that she wants the radio on, but you say, "Too bad, I'm not turning it on," she probably quiets down. How nice to have quietness, especially when you are tired and fed up. But this is not validating parenting and, in the long run, makes your job as a parent harder. Telling your child that you understand that she would like the radio on but you still aren't going to turn it on would be the better approach. The good news is that validating your child is more likely to result in her centering herself and becoming more cooperative in the hours to come. Validating parenting continues to cultivate a safe space for your child and you.

Parents Find Reality Too Hard to Accept

Sometimes children express an emotion that triggers feelings in parents that they don't want to feel. For example, when your daughter is upset that she didn't make the cheerleading team, you hurt for her. To stop your own hurting, you invalidate her feelings, perhaps by saying it wasn't worth her time anyway or that she should be happy she didn't make the team because all the girls on the squad are mean anyway.

Maybe your son goes to a birthday party where the parents have arranged for a famous baseball player to work with the boys on a professional diamond. Or your daughter's best friend is given designer boots for her birthday. When your children tell you how wonderful their friends' parents are and that they want the same, you may invalidate them because you feel bad about being unable to afford such gifts or are unwilling to buy them. You may say, "Don't even think about it," or "That's ridiculous to want such things," which may make you feel better but tells your child that what she feels is wrong. If reality is just allowed to be, then suffering is next to impossible. The Buddhist faith has this concept down pat. If we accept reality, then the painful feelings are not nearly as powerful. If you accept your child's painful feelings as they are, then you are less likely to suffer by trying to change the feelings. Just accept them.

Here's another example: Your son struggles with math and isn't going to pass. You don't want to accept that he has a problem learning the material, so you invalidate him by telling him he's not trying hard enough. Think of how it will affect him to carry those words with him, when he believes he is trying as hard as he can. If you accept reality, that he may have a learning disability or may simply not have an aptitude for math, then it will free you to actually be effective for him and get the necessary help that he needs. It may mean that you grieve some. If your child has learning problems, you may fear that he will suffer in life. This may be true, but nonacceptance will ensure that he doesn't get the help he needs and suffers more.

There are more serious issues as well. Some children struggle with chronic illnesses, such as diabetes or cancer. Some children have lost a limb, or have lost a parent. Validating that the struggle is difficult acknowledges the truth. Acknowledging that your child's life will be different because of the illness, loss, or disability can be heartbreaking but is necessary.

Parents Don't Want Their Children to Go through What They Went Through

A well-intentioned dad or mom could easily be guilty of this sort of invalidating behavior. Consider the dad who was on the wrestling team in middle school. His son does not want to be a wrestler and believes he won't be happy participating in this contact sport. The dad, however, feels that he suffered as a child because he never wrestled as well as he wanted to. He spends hours working with his son to help him learn a sport his son doesn't like. Another scenario would be if the dad becomes very disappointed at his son's disinterest in wrestling and makes negative statements about it. Both responses invalidate the son's feelings about wrestling. The son believes he will be happier if he doesn't wrestle, but the father feels differently, and his behavior and words invalidate the son's feelings.

Pushing your children into groups of friends because of your perceptions about the popularity or desirability of the people involved is an easy mistake to make. Often your child can read his peers better than you can. What may have worked for you in elementary or middle school is not necessarily what's right for your child. Our kids often know better than we do about their needs, and we just need to listen and consider their viewpoint. Reagan, aged seven, is invited to a party in which all the first-graders will be loaded into a limousine and taken to play paintball, followed by a pool party and a sleepover. Reagan's mom always wanted to be part of the popular group when she was younger. Imagine her dismay when her son says he doesn't want to go. His befuddled mother asks him why, and Reagan responds, "Because that guy is mean, and I have seen him push his sister down on the playground at school." His mother almost tells him to go anyway because of the limousine ride and the fact that all the popular kids will be there. Instead she stops, validates her son on his character, and takes him out that night herself. She sets aside her desires and expectations and allows her child to be himself. That is validation.

Further, be careful of invalidating your child's feelings while telling him you love him. If your child brings home a bad test score, you might say, "It's okay; I still love you," but in doing so, you might imply that even in this awful situation, you still love him. You are making your love for him contingent on his behavior in a potentially scary and invalidating way. The implication is that although he has performed terribly and the situation is very bad, you love him anyway, but someday he may perform so poorly that you may not love him anymore. Is a low math grade really a reason not to love your son? No. If his test grade is low and he is sad about it, try to find the silver lining for yourself. At least he cares. Use this opportunity to validate that he cares and to validate that he confided in you about his sadness, and then get him a tutor. That would be effective as well as validating. Also, you, as his parent, have the adult perspective that failing math will not result in a failed life, but somewhere inside of you, you may worry that he feels that. Be careful not to even connect the two. It's doubtful that your son has.

Parents Set Their Children Up for Success

For many reasons, it scares some parents to think that their child might fail at something. They may fear that the child's failure reflects on them negatively as parents or perhaps that if the child fails at turning in a homework assignment, she will be labeled as a slacker for life and be treated differently at school because of it. Sometimes parents fear that the child doesn't understand the importance of school and won't get into a good college without their help. Most children start out wanting to do their own work, but their parents' actions may teach them that their work isn't acceptable. The more their parents step in and do their work for them, the less masterful they feel about their own work. After a while, they can't do the work. A first-grade teacher at a Houston elementary school said that often when her students are given an assignment appropriate for first grade, the work that comes back is that of an adult who obviously completed the assignment for the child. The teacher explained that she always gives higher grades to work actually completed by first-graders, even if it doesn't compare in excellence to work that was obviously completed by the parents. She also shared that parents call her to complain about the grades given. At this point she explains that had the first-grader actually done the work, she would have given the grade the work commands, but it is clear that the child did not do the work, which results in a lower grade. The message you want to give as a parent is to validate that your child's successes and failures are hers, and by each success and failure, she will grow, further enabling her to have a successful adulthood. If parents continue to pick up the pieces for their children, the children won't have the skills of accepting both success and failure and won't develop the skills they need, thus ensuring the very outcome the parents fear.

Some parents argue with teachers about grades and lie to protect their children from failure. Their fears drive them to do whatever they can to protect the child (and in some cases themselves) from failures. The child's weaknesses and lack of effort may not even be acknowledged. Some parents do all they can to protect their children from actual consequences at school, while simultaneously berating them for not completing projects and homework. This inconsistent message completely confuses the child. The goal is to raise successful children. Success comes from hard work and practice at coping with necessary failures.

Validation is never about pretending or lying. Part of validating your child is recognizing his need to do his own work and use his own skills to learn, to receive extra help at times, and yes, to fail and recover from the failure. Learning what he can do, learning to fail and try again, and recognizing his strengths and weaknesses are part of your child's learning who he is and accepting himself. Validating behavior is letting your child do the work and take responsibility for it.

When not allowed to fail or to do his own work, the child doesn't learn how to cope with failure or develop skills to cope with the real world. Unfortunately the ability to manage failure is one of the skills needed to persevere toward goals. Failing also teaches children how to be flexible and to tolerate disappointment.

Meredith really wants to be a singer. She has the drive, the motivation, and the desire but lacks enough skill to make the choir. She practices and practices but still never makes the cut. Imagine her dismay when each time she auditions, she is rejected. She is sick about it. What her parents need to do is to validate her efforts, validate how proud of her they are for her work ethic and determination. They have taught her that doing your best does not always mean that you win, but you always know in your heart that you did your best, which is an accomplishment. When a child knows that she did her best, it's a good feeling, even if it means that she loses. Meredith is crushed, but still has a good feeling about her efforts, so she can feel validated.

Another example is Misty. Misty hurts her wrist playing volleyball and isn't able to type the history paper that's due in two days. Her mother volunteers to type it from Misty's dictation. Unfortunately, Misty hasn't read the information she needs to complete the paper. Her mother fusses at her but fills in the information and corrects Misty's grammar. Her mother, who worries that Misty won't get into the more competitive high school if she doesn't get good grades in middle school, makes some other changes as well. She reasons that it's "just this one time." But Misty always seems to have a reason she can't do her homework on her own. Misty begins to believe that she isn't capable of doing well, and she fears doing her own work. Her mother doesn't realize that she is invalidating Misty's competency and mastery by taking over a task that belongs to her daughter.

Loving parents often don't want their children to exhibit feelings that they believe could inhibit or diminish their success in life. Hatred, jealousy, and hostility expressed by a child may chill parents to the bone, so that they resort to shaming or punishment in hopes that these emotions will dissipate. These responses do not work and, in fact, can cause problems, such as rebellious, anxious, and guilt-ridden children. It's important that children be able to express these negative emotions, even when they say, "I hate you, Mommy." Tolerating these emotions shows the child that the parent doesn't fear these emotions, that the child can learn to manage them, and that these emotions are normal. By accepting such emotions, the parent can foster in the child the ability to live without having these emotions control his life.

Parents Are Afraid of Failing as Parents

When you held that tiny infant, you vowed that her life would be better than yours because you would give her a better life than you had. You want the best for her, and you work hard to do a better job than even your parents did. You also try to be an educated, positive parent. As your children grow, you begin to see their perceived failures—such as feeling chubby or sad, not thriving in school, or not being in the popular crowd—as your own failures. Parents with the best of intentions don't want those negative situations to be true, so they tell their children that they are wrong, that they have so much potential they are not living up to and need to try harder, that their lives are so much easier than their parents' that their parents had to walk five miles in the snow to catch the bus and these children are driven to school and therefore should be happy.

It's hard to accept that even if you do your best as a parent, your children may not be as successful, popular, or happy as you want them to be. What we forget is that these feelings in children usually pass. Your child will be success-ful and happy and will have friends, but often, in the moment, that's hard for them (and you) to see. This is why we validate, not agree. It helps keep us grounded so that we can respond appropriately as well. Validating how your child feels will help him move on, and you too.

Parents Want Their Children to Behave Normally

Each child is different. One child in a group of siblings or in a classroom may be more sensitive than another. A child may be more sensitive than her par-ents are. The difficult thing is that parents tend to use their own worldly experience (or that of parenting other children) to determine the boundaries of normal experience. If you are sensitive to pain, you understand and accept strong reactions to skinned knees and pinched fingers. If you have a high tolerance for pain, you may see a child's perceived "overreaction" to a sprained ankle or skinned knee as being attention seeking or overdramatic. Since you don't want to raise a "drama queen" or a "wimp," you may invalidate your child's reactions so that she can learn to be "normal," like the other children.

Stella Chess and Alexander Thomas (1986) assert that children are born with different temperaments, some more sensitive than others. If your child is sensitive and you aren't particularly sensitive, it may be difficult to understand your child's reactions. Among siblings, if two of the kids aren't emotionally sensitive but the third one is incredibly sensitive and emotionally vulnerable, then the third child's reactions may seem even more extreme than the other two's, making him seem like the "problem child." Because your experience with emotional reactions gives you your sense of what's normal, your sensitive child's intense reactions may seem fake or exaggerated. In fact, that child may be expressing his feelings the way he experiences them, but they make no sense to you. This is one of the hardest tasks for parents. When one child seems "different" from the others, it can appear to his parents that there's something wrong with him. Learning to recognize emotional vulnerability within this child is the key to validating him. There is absolutely nothing wrong with him, and he will probably grow up to be an incredibly sensitive and loving husband someday, as long as his sensitivity is not invalidated while he is young.

Parents Know Their Children's Habits

Maybe you have one child who typically does not put away her toys and another who does. You have a reward system for completing the task. One day you walk into their playroom, and all the toys are put away. You compliment the child who usually puts the toys away, and he accepts the compliment. The other child argues that she put the toys away this time. The first child insists that he did. You could naturally say to the other child, "You never put the toys away," and be concerned that she is lying. What if she really did put the toys away this one time? Your response would be significantly invalidating.

Sometimes parents impose roles on their children, such as the smart child, the child who lies, or the caring child. These roles may be based on the parents' past experience with the child or with someone the child reminds them of. Seeing a child in a certain way because of an assigned role, with no room for the child to behave differently than you expect, is invalidating.

Parents' Emotions Overwhelm Them

As a parent, you can easily become angry, sad, or anxious as a result of your child's emotions. It's also easy to try to reduce your anxiety over these emotions and react to them in ways that aren't validating to your children. If you have spent all day setting up a birthday party for your child, who then complains that she really wanted a chocolate cake, not vanilla, even though yesterday she wanted vanilla, you may be tempted to tell her quite angrily that she is an ungrateful little girl who doesn't deserve the great party you put together and that this is the last party she will get. Most parents have experienced this, and most have probably invalidated in this very way. If you find that your emotions are getting the better of you, maybe it's time for you to step back and examine your own life. Are you overstressed, overdoing for your child, or building resentments in other relationships that affect your parenting, or are you downright overwhelmed by the entire task of parenting? If so, it might be good for your child if you took inventory of your own emotions and burdens in order to parent more effectively. We believe this is key.

Again, if your emotions overwhelm your parenting, it may be time to step back and ask yourself why you are having this response. In the previous example, is the daughter being unreasonable? Yes, probably, but why do you have that response? You may remember your own birthday, when sugar was in short supply and you couldn't even have a cake, much less a choice about what kind of cake. Remember, thoughts and experiences of yours have nothing to do with your daughter. She doesn't have that same reality. Validate her indecisiveness and make it clear that she is getting vanilla but that she doesn't have to be happy about it. Tell her that you love her and want her to have a special birthday party but that the cake will remain vanilla.

Tessa is a fifth-grader who is desperate to make the cheerleading team at her middle school the next year. This is a difficult goal to achieve, and Tessa works hard for months to try to make the team. The day of the tryouts comes and Tessa makes the team. She is ecstatic but also very fearful. It means much responsibility and time away from her peers and schoolwork. As excited as Tessa is, she is also a little anxious. When she expresses this to her mother, her mother becomes irate and feels completely overwhelmed at her daughter's expression of her feelings after all the mother has done to help her child be successful. The mother focuses on the expense of the private lessons, the time and energy away from the family while Tessa was practicing, the emotions leading up to finding out she made the team, and the emotional drain the mother feels. It becomes more about the mother's emotions than about Tessa. All Tessa needs to hear is that her anxiety and nervousness make sense. She is not a stitch ungrateful, but that's what her mother perceives in Tessa's expression.

Many can relate to Tessa's mother. Tessa is like so many kids out there who just want a safe place to vent. This is one reason private-practice therapists have so many sessions a week just for teenagers who need a nonjudgmental place to express their feelings without having others emotionally attach to what they say. Starting to be a nonjudgmental sounding board for your child's emotions will change the very nature of your relationship with your child. Start with the emotions that are easier for you to accept, and see if you can graduate to the ones that are more difficult to accept. It will get easier. It may also just be that your child needs a safe place to vent and doesn't even want you to say a word at all. Just simply asking your children what they need may be a good place to start.

Parents Are in a Hurry

Just before she has to leave for school, Lucy typically gets upset with her mother, who has to get to work on time. Lucy can't find her homework that she spent hours doing the night before. School has not been easy for her. Lucy and her mom have made it Lucy's responsibility to put her homework in her blue notebook right after completing it and put the blue notebook into her backpack right away. Unfortunately, Lucy does not consistently do this. As a matter of fact, Lucy does not consistently do anything. She is more distracted than her siblings were at the same age, which often frustrates her mother. Can you picture your own reaction? Even if Lucy just couldn't find a sweater she wanted to wear and they were rushed for time, her mother would be vulnerable to invalidating her. Take a moment to think about your reaction here. Being in a hurry, out of control of their own emotions, tired, or ill can be why parents don't respond in validating ways. The validating thing to do might be to tell Lucy that you understand that it's upsetting to her to not have her sweater or her homework, but you cannot help her look for it now. Now it's time to go to school, with or without the homework or the sweater. This also might mean that your child might fail at something at school, but allowing that failure is what helps children to learn to be successful on their own. In this situation, validating her feelings, while not altering your behavior, can be some of the best teaching that you can give your child.

Parents also have real-world demands they must meet. Lucy's mother simply needs to be at work on time, this morning especially, and cannot wait for Lucy to search. Lucy needs to learn to wait until after school to find what she wants. Learning to wait is also a skill for children to learn. The age of the child will affect how long he can wait, but teaching patience in this way is a step toward reducing impulsive responses. Sometimes validating means stating that the situation isn't perfect and you can't do what you wish you could do in that moment.

Parents Forget That Children's Brains Are Still Developing

For some time, researchers thought that brain growth occurred mainly before eighteen months of age. Later, researchers learned that the brain is still developing well into the teen years (NIMH 2010).

Many times parents and teachers ask children and teenagers, "Did you not think about the consequences? You knew you would get into trouble, get caught, break something, or get hurt. You never think! Tell me why you keep doing this!" Children cannot tell you they are still impulsive beings who do not think ahead because their brains are not fully developed. Wouldn't that help defuse our emotional response if they could? Kids don't know this about themselves. They just act, and many times they feel that their behavior was out of character for them when reflecting on the behavior.

Children and teens can know right from wrong and have a strong moral code but be unable to make decisions about their behavior based on that strong moral code. They also can't tell you why. The *prefrontal cortex*, which is the rational part of the brain, the part that understands consequences of actions and makes decisions about behavior based on that understanding, may not be fully developed, and its connections with other parts of the brain are not as solid as an adult's, even until age eighteen (Packard 2007). The preteen may say, "I don't know why I poured purple hair dye on Jason's blond hair while he was sleeping. It was just a joke." On hearing this, parents go ballistic: "What do you mean you don't know why you went to Tristan's house when his parents weren't home?" "Why did you decide to wrap the house of the minister who doesn't have a sense of humor?" and so on.

Validation in this sense is really about recognizing what your child can and can't do developmentally. Validation of the fact that your child's brain is immature means that you accept that he is not ready to live without your supervising and checking up on him.

Wrapping Up

As you can see, there are many reasons why parents invalidate. It's easy to invalidate, and we all do it at some point or another. But there's a high cost to our children if we do it on a regular basis. To reiterate, be careful about telling your children that the way they feel is wrong or that they don't really know what they feel.

When we invalidate our children, we're telling them they need to be different than they are. While we don't mean to do so, we are saying that they are wrong as people and that their instincts and feelings are wrong.

Chapter 5

Ways Parents Invalidate

In the previous chapter we discussed why parents invalidate their children. To change this behavior, it's important to recognize how invalidation occurs. In this chapter we will discuss several common ways parents invalidate children. Because we can be blind to our own behavior, we suggest discussing these behaviors with a trusted adult who you know will be honest with you.

Blaming

A common belief is that if something goes wrong, then someone must be to blame. Sometimes we even look for someone to blame when things go wrong. This can often be the child. "You're the reason your father left," "No one wants to date anyone with a kid," and "I would have been an actress, but I chose to be your mother instead, and you don't appreciate all the sacrifices I've made for you," are all invalidating statements. But how are they invalidating? In these examples, it isn't feelings or thoughts that are invalidated—it's the whole person. The person's existence is the problem, and the child becomes wrong for existing. Blame can also show up as judgment of a child for something she may or may not have done wrong. For example, Betsy, a fifth-grader, is supposed to tell her mother that she needs to be at school early so that she can be featured in the morning announcements. Betsy forgets to let her mother know in advance and informs her in the morning that she needs to be at school thirty minutes early that day. Betsy's mother is unprepared for this and becomes stressed and anxious about getting Betsy to school on time. She then turns to Betsy and says, "If you were more organized with your time and less of a slacker, we would not be in this mess right now." Betsy already knows she is wrong, but her mother's shame and blame make it worse. Her mother could be more effective with her by making Betsy miss her time on the announcements since she is not prepared for it. This would teach Betsy with negative consequences, rather than by blaming her.

Requiring a child to take responsibility differs from blaming. Taking responsibility is about a specific behavior, not the whole person. For example, you might say, "This lamp broke because you played ball in the house when you knew it was against the rules." This is pointing out cause and effect, or responsibility. Children are continually learning about cause-and-effect relationships. Pointing out how a behavior leads to a result can be helpful and is not invalidating. Betsy needs to take responsibility for her schedule, no doubt, but blame won't help her do that.

Ignoring

Not responding to a child's expressions, without explaining why you aren't responding, makes a strong statement. It's a nonverbal way of saying that the child or his words are unimportant. Responding "Sure," or "Uh-huh," to your child's request is invalidating. Telling a child that you don't have time for him right now without ever going back and addressing his concerns or questions is invalidating. Telling a child that you will listen to him in a minute, without following through on that commitment, is invalidating. Just not paying attention because you are too busy or for any other reason is invalidating. We all have times when we are too busy to listen to a child's story or to look at something that's interesting to a child. Explaining that you can't pay attention right now is a better choice than pretending to or offering lip service.

Speaking as If the Child Isn't Present

Most of us can remember adults discussing something we did as children in a way that implied that we had no feelings of embarrassment or weren't entitled to privacy. Our most embarrassing moments might have entertained the bunko or bridge group. Perhaps your parents told the story, sometimes pushing you away, saying, "You don't mind if I tell my friends about this, do you?" or maybe, "Oh, that's nothing to be embarrassed about." Information about our bodies was often the focus, such as, "Can you believe Missy is only ten and already getting breasts?" or "Mikey took forever to toilet train. I think he was almost three and still in diapers." We hated some of those stories, although sometimes we enjoyed being the center of attention. The invalidation comes from sharing the child's private experiences, experiences he may not want shared, and doing so as if his feelings do not matter.

Sometimes the issue of speaking as if the child were not present happens within the family. When they're angry, some mothers talk to themselves about how angry they are and how unbelievably selfish the child is. They walk around the house banging pots and slamming cabinet doors, obviously furious and complaining aloud about the child's behavior. Some parents hold discussions in front of the child while ignoring the child. For example, Ashley wants to go to a music camp in Boston, far away from where her parents live in Texas. Without any assistance from the adults in her life, she applies; practices for the audition, which is held in her home city; and is accepted. Her parents are shocked to learn that she has been accepted. They proceed to talk to each other about how ludicrous it would be to allow her to go to Boston. The father is angry with the mother because she took Ashley to the audition and hasn't canceled the application. Red in the face, he tells his wife that Ashley will never be successful there, so he won't allow her to go in the first place. He complains that it would be a waste of good money. They speak about Ashley as if she is not even present. Ashley just stands there and feels invisible. She feels that she has shown plenty of initiative and effort to get there and could be successful, but now she is ignored and invalidated. Her confidence in her musical ability is shaken such that she stops applying to any music programs.

Discussing Children's Private Feelings Openly with Others

This way of invalidating children is related to the previous one. The main difference is that instead of talking in front of the children, parents share private information about their children with other adults in ways that the children overhear. A little girl has trouble with wetting the bed. As embarrassing as this is to the girl privately, she often hears her mom discussing this problem with her friends, many of whom are her own friends' mothers. This is mortifying to the girl. She confides in her mother about something embarrassing and shameful and is appalled to learn that her mom is sharing this personal information about her with others in the town. This ultimately leads her to distrust her mom as a confidant.

This issue is a difficult one. Parents need the support of their friends and have the right to share with them. Often it's the most embarrassing situations for children that parents need the most support with. Concerning potentially embarrassing information, you need to choose your confidant carefully, perhaps someone who doesn't have children the same age and who is very good at keeping information to herself.

Ignoring Children's Choices

Sally has wanted to play football all of her life, but her mother refuses. She tells Sally that football is for boys, implying that there's something wrong with Sally for wanting to play that sport. Sally obliges her mom and plays soccer instead, though she dislikes soccer, and is not very good at it. She harbors ill will toward her mother for not letting her do what she wants. What her mom doesn't realize is that the desire to play football is, for Sally, simply an act of showing her independence. She is pushing appropriate boundaries with her mother and asserting her own likes and desires.

Telling your child that he enjoys something when he doesn't is invalidating. Jack has liked eggs all of his life, even to the point of learning to make them himself by the time he is seven. His parents are very impressed by this and talk about it proudly among their friends! Their son is seven and scrambles eggs. As time goes on, Jack stops liking eggs. His parents cannot understand that, and they ask him repeatedly what's wrong with him that he no longer likes eggs. They go so far as to try to force him to eat eggs, despite the fact that he has told him that his internal experience around eggs has changed such that they now make him feel sick. His parents later learn that Jack is actually allergic to eggs and that they truly do make him sick. His parents are able to validate that, but only because there is external evidence to confirm Jack's internal impressions. This is not an example of validation, but exactly the opposite.

Just listening to what your children want is a good start to becoming a validating parent. Hearing what they need is half of being able to give it to them.

Pushing the Child to Be Better than the Parent

Twelve-year-old Jake has the opportunity to attend a special art camp for gifted children. He also has the opportunity to go on vacation with his best friend's family, which means he would miss art camp. Jake is clear that he isn't that interested in art and really wants to go on vacation with his friend. Jake's father wants his son to have opportunities that he did not have, such as a better education and special classes to get ahead. He hopes for Jake to have a better life than he had as a child, but the result ends up being negative. His dad pushes Jake to make the "smart" choice, the one that would make him "better." While Jake's dad is a good parent, he is hurting his child. Over the years, he pushes Jake to paint and draw every evening and weekend so that he can become a better and better artist. The problem with this is that Jake's desires are invalidated when he does what pleases his dad. He is learning to put someone else's desires for him over his own. Imagine what this will mean for his life. He may have a drug-using friend down the road who wants him to join in and will be unhappy with him if he doesn't. Jake will have no practice or template for meeting his own needs if he continually meets other people's needs. Further, pushing your kids to be different from how they are ultimately sets them up for possible resentments toward you later in life. Finding a balance between encouragement and acceptance is a way to keep from pushing your child into something that he doesn't want.

Not Letting Children Succeed or Fail

Ainsley keeps forgetting to bring her completed homework to school. Her mom, not wanting her to fail, drives Ainsley's homework to her school whenever she forgets it. But one day, her mom neglects to bring the forgotten homework, and Ainsley gets a grade of zero. If it had been this way all along, that if she forgets her homework, then she gets a zero, Ainsley couldn't be angry at her mom for not bringing it to her. It's Ainsley's job to remember to bring her homework, not her mother's, but her mother has set up a world in which Ainsley does not fail—ironically, to Ainsley's detriment.

Putting Children in Situations before They Are Ready

Jeannette's mother sees great potential in her daughter's ability to compete in gymnastics. The coaches see it too, so they all agree to put her daughter on a competitive gymnastics team, despite the fact that Jeannette expresses a strong desire not to compete. The child knows that she doesn't have the drive to succeed. She knows that the competitions will be intense and that she is not prepared to handle the stress. She also wants to just hang out with her friends! As time goes on, this child grows more and more depressed, feeling inadequate in her ability to compete, which leads to feelings of inadequacy across the board in her life. She is not ready to compete and makes that clear to her mom up front. Her mother feels that it's best not to listen to her daughter's internal response, and so she listens to the coaches and her own desires instead. Sometimes children do need to be pushed out of their comfort zones, but this is different. This girl knows she does not want to be a competitor. She wants to take gymnastics lightly and have more of a social life. She tries to tell her mom but is not heard, which is invalidating.

Fearing Angering or Disappointing Children

A single mom, Janet is doing her best at bringing up her daughter, Tori, and she knows it. Many times, what Tori wants to do wins out over what Janet thinks is best for her, because Janet feels tremendous guilt over working full-time and not being married to Tori's father. This leads to a cycle in which Tori wants something, doesn't get it, and throws a fit, and then Janet gives in. This actually sets up a pattern of behavior that Janet finds very difficult to get out of, which means that she continually walks on eggshells trying to control Tori's emotions by giving her what she wants in all situations. Janet does not want to make her daughter sad or mad, so she continually gives her what she wants. Validating parenting means that we *parent*. Janet is no longer parenting. She is not willing to have her daughter be sad, which actually does a disservice to Tori. Tori needs to learn to tolerate disappointment and sadness in order to grow into a fully functioning adult.

Parents sometimes struggle with the desire to accept only positive feelings in their children. Not wanting Tori to be sad over being excluded from the girls' cotillion that all of the popular kids were invited to join, Janet offers to pay for highlights, a personal trainer, and a new cell phone so that Tori can feel that she fits in with all of the other girls in the sixth grade. Janet is encouraging Tori not to hurt and is teaching her to find ways to mask what she actually feels if her emotions are unpleasant. The problem with this approach is that humans are hardwired to feel both good and bad, and masking the bad or not allowing Tori to feel negative emotions sets her up for a lifetime of self-invalidation.

Putting Children's Desires and Choices at the Bottom of the List

Let's say that you have a son who wants to wear pink. Whatever he wants, right? Not always. Many parents would feel uncomfortable with that. This discomfort may push you to tell your son that what he desires is wrong and that men do not wear pink. Making a stink over it could possibly create problems that were never there in the first place. By putting your child's needs first, as long as they are not self-destructive or from a spoiled stance will be most validating. Putting your son's need first will allow him to be able to fully grow into the adult you hope he will be. This example illustrates how what society validates is sometimes different from what individuals may think and feel. Depending on the school, your son's classmates may not accept his wearing pink. Conveying information about how society may view actions, thoughts, and feelings can help your child if you do so in a neutral manner. While, as a parent, you see nothing wrong with his love of pink, other people in your child's world may not agree.

Putting a child's choices or desires above those of the rest of the family sends the message that he should get what he wants, regardless of the cost to others. No child should have his choices ignored, nor should a child's desires dominate. It is a challenge to find a balance, but it is possible.

Laughing at Children's Ideas or Feelings

Your eight-year-old daughter asks for an expensive MP3 player for Christmas, one that streams movies, records workout times, plays music, and even brushes her teeth! She wants this very badly, because many of her friends have it. In her opinion, its cost is not a problem, because Santa will deliver it with all of her other goodies at Christmas! Not wanting to set your daughter up for disappointment, you laugh and tell her that it's ridiculous to ask for such a gift. You say that Santa will never bring that to her because it is too expensive and inappropriate for an eight-year-old. While you have the best of intentions and are trying to prepare her for disappointment, you are doing your daughter a disservice. Although you are protecting her from shattered expectations on Christmas morning, you are also invalidating her thoughts. A more validating response would be "That's an amazing gadget. I can understand why you would like to have one. Santa may see that as a gift that you can get when you are older. Let's see what happens"

Minimizing or Magnifying Children's Feelings, Thoughts, and Behaviors

Nine-year-old Chelsea declares that she doesn't like chocolate cake. Her mother, who worked hard all week and brought the cake home to celebrate the weekend, responds angrily to Chelsea's stated preference: "You liked chocolate cake two weeks ago. Why are you being so difficult? Do you just want to ruin our time together?" Chelsea is shocked. She doesn't understand why liking or disliking chocolate cake is important. Her mother has magnified her feelings from a neutral dessert preference to the idea that Chelsea doesn't want to spend time together.

Minimizing a child's feelings is invalidating as well. Twelve-year-old Amy is in tears because she has a pimple on her face the night of a basketball game she is attending. "I feel so ugly," she cries. Her mother replies, "You're being so ridiculous. No one will even see it." To Amy, the pimple is a big deal. Amy feels that her mother doesn't understand and refuses to talk with her anymore about the issue. It also minimizes a child's feelings when you offer a solution. It would be invalidating for Amy's mom to offer pimple medicine or a trip to the dermatologist to fix her feelings of ugliness. Just stating that you can understand that the pimple is a big deal and that she feels ugly would be enough. More than a solution to her problem, Amy wants to be heard.

Invalidating Comments and Situations

We've discussed some ways that parents invalidate their children. Now let's consider some specific invalidating statements that parents might inadvertently make.

"You could not possibly be hungry again."

"Do you want to be a girl?" (said with hostility to a boy in a pink shirt).

"I don't know what you are crying about. Didn't I tell you this would happen?"

"You never listen" (absolute adverbs, such as "always" and "never," tend to be invalidating).

"A first-grader could do better than that!"

"Why can't you be more like _____?"

"I bet your sister would have made that field goal."

"No, I'm not mad" (when you are).

"There's nothing wrong with your socks" (when your child says the socks itch).

"You will eat what I tell you to eat."

"You do like broccoli" (when your child says he doesn't).

"I can't believe you are scared of that little dog."

"Of course you want to go to the party; the most popular kids will be there."

"Don't be scared; he won't hurt you."

"Don't be silly; you have plenty of friends at school."

"You have to hug and kiss Grandma. Don't be rude."

"Eat your food. Don't be ugly."

"You're going to get fat."

"Now, you eat what they give you and don't complain. They can't make something special just for you."

"I don't have time for this" (said in a demeaning way).

"Uh-huh" (while busy doing something else).

"I'd just like to see you try it" (sarcasm).

"You are not this upset about that!" (minimalization).

"Get up from there, and stop being such a baby!"

"I cannot believe you are so selfish."

"If you just talk to people, you will make friends."

"If you practice more, you will get to play. You are as good as any of the other players, but you don't practice."

A behavioral rule in psychology says that to pay attention to any behavior is to increase the likelihood that the behavior will recur, provided the person engaging in the behavior likes the attention (Zastrow and Kirst-Ashman 2010). If every time your child says he feels ill, you give him lots of attention and special food that he loves, and this doesn't happen at other times, then you are increasing the likelihood that he will say that he is ill when he really isn't. Why doesn't validation increase acting out, giving excuses, or lying?

Remember the mother who told her daughter Jessica that she wasn't hungry, even though her daughter clearly stated that she was? When you, as a parent, are concerned about your child's health, about teasing, or about him or her becoming overweight, what do you do? There are several options.

First of all, the child says she is hungry, so that needs to be validated. "I understand that you still feel hungry. You know, it takes about twenty minutes for the stomach to let the brain know it has had food. Let's wait twenty minutes and then see if you are still hungry." If the child is still hungry at that point, you could offer more food options. If this is a continual issue, an appointment with a pediatrician might be advisable.

Perhaps Jessica is not really hungry but is using this tactic to ask for a special treat, like ice cream. Of course, offering more broccoli won't satisfy her. Lecturing Jessica about the dangers of eating sweets and the importance of not gaining weight would likely be damaging, by turning certain foods into "bad foods." Restricting certain foods in this way then creates a love-hate relationship with those foods, potentially setting up a cycle of overindulging and restricting.

You may be annoyed by your child's indirect way of asking for ice cream. Perhaps looking at why she does not ask directly would be helpful. If your reaction to a request for sweets is to become upset, then she will try to find a way around this reaction. Maybe reevaluating your reactions would be helpful. Maybe your response needs to be a simple yes or no based on facts, not fears: no to ice cream because dinner will be served in a few minutes, or no to ice cream because it's healthier to eat the basic food groups first. It could also be a big step to say yes to desserts, making them available without restriction after meals, so that their appeal would diminish with their greater availability. It may be that the very best response is to put no restrictions on food so that the child doesn't focus on scarcity and may then be able to attend to her internal signals of hunger and fullness. Validating her ability to know her own signals will help her develop a healthy use of food as fuel for her body.

Part of validating your child is acknowledging what's true and authentic. If a child is repeatedly crying or teasing a sibling and it seems to you that he wants your attention, then address this with him. Acknowledging the true feeling behind the emotion is a key part of validation. Our experience is that when a child's true emotion and experience is validated, the emotion tends to dissipate more quickly, and efforts to express emotions in inappropriate ways cease. Validation reinforces genuine, authentic, direct communication. In addition, when you use your validating parenting skills, your child receives attention for positive growth and development and does not need to seek attention in unhealthy ways.

Wrapping Up

The majority of parents work hard at parenting and want to be the best parents possible. Yet we're all human. In this chapter, we looked at some of the very human ways that even dedicated parents may sometimes invalidate their children.

Chapter 6

Validating Parenting in Depth

We've discussed what validation is, what it isn't, the reasons why parents invalidate, and some ways they invalidate. You've been introduced to the skills parents need to develop to successfully apply validating parenting. Now it's time to learn more specific skills. In this chapter we'll discuss the levels of validation (Linehan 1993), which we've modified slightly to apply to parenting. We will also provide examples of how to apply validation at each level.

Levels of Validation

One of the key ideas that Marsha Linehan (1997) has contributed to the study of validation is the different levels of validation, which are more like different types of validation, without one level being considered higher than another. With the exception of level 1, the levels are independent of each other but not mutually exclusive.

Level 1: Showing Interest and Being Present

This level of validation identified by Linehan (1997) simply means that as a parent, you show up, pay attention, and stay awake to your child and what she is doing and telling you. Acting as if you are interested, when in fact other thoughts or activities are distracting you, is invalidating to your child. For example, if you pick up your child from school and act as if you want to hear about her day but are busy answering text messages and e-mails, you are actually not showing up for your child. This is the simplest of the levels but the one that's often missed.

One of the most basic ways of validating someone is to be there. Attending school functions, games, and birthday parties tells your child that he is important to you. Being present means that you are paying attention to your child, rather than hanging out in the parking lot talking with friends or chatting in the bleachers. It means you aren't preoccupied with an overly busy schedule or the argument you had with your spouse this morning.

"Watch me, Mommy! Watch me," is a common request from children, as is "Did you see me, Daddy?" "I just made that hook shot right over the top" comes from older children. As a child, being paid attention means that you matter.

At a talent show for middle-school students, one mother spent the whole time talking with friends in the lobby. When her daughter was on stage, she looked around for her mother and couldn't find her. Her face showed her disappointment. Being physically present is not sufficient. You must be emotionally and cognitively present as well. Kids are very well aware when we parents are not present. They can read it in our body language and in our attention to the details that they share. It's deflating to children to recognize that they are not as important to their parents as they would like to feel.

Being present means to actually be there in both good and bad times. When Lisa is crying, you are there to hold her. When Andy is upset because he didn't make the baseball team, you are there to just be with him. When Julio throws a temper tantrum in church, you are there to help him get his feelings under control. That would not be the time to try to fix the situation or tell your child what he did wrong. Again, being a safe haven for your child to be himself is an important part of being a parent. One parent of children from elementary-school to high-school age sometimes did not know what to do when her children started venting intense feelings to her. She finally decided to ask her kids. When one child shared some "drama" about her day, the mother started out by asking the child if she wanted her to just listen and validate or to offer solutions. This transformed the dynamic between this parent and her children. She found that most times, they did not want solutions; they just wanted to be heard and validated. This can be a relief to parents as well.

Parents always have so much to do. We plan parties, participate in the PTA, remember our neighbors' birthdays, cook, shop for groceries, take care of our parents, do financial planning, work, and on and on. Sometimes we just don't have enough time to really pay attention to our children, so we wash dishes and nod while they tell us about their day. That's invalidating. Children can feel when they are getting our attention and when they are only part of a multitasking event.

Try it for yourself. First involve yourself in some activity, don't make eye contact with your child, and half-listen to her while nodding or asking routine questions now and then. Now, stop. Give your full attention to your child for a few minutes. Really listen, making eye contact. Ask what you really would like to know. Then go back to your activity.

It's interesting that you will probably finish your task faster and do it better if you give it your full attention rather than split your attention. You will probably find that your child will be less needy in the long run as well. Plus, if your child knows that waiting means he gets your full attention, he will become better at waiting until you are finished with something else. Otherwise, he remains unsatisfied and keeps trying to get your full attention, because that means he is worthwhile and valuable. Your full attention and interest validate him as a person.

Is it possible to be present without showing interest? Yes. You could be a silent observer, with your attention and thoughts on what your child does or says, without indicating that you are interested. That would be listening and observing without feeling. Most times, you must combine being present with showing interest. Pay careful attention and show that you care about what your child does and says. There are few situations in which you would want to merely be present. If your child is completely emotional, throwing a huge temper tantrum to the point where he cannot listen to you, then being present and showing as little emotion as you can manage is the best option. Your job at such times is not to add emotion to the situation, throwing fuel on the fire, so to speak, but to contain your child and keep him safe.

Showing interest without being present is impossible. To do so would be to fake interest, which would not be validating. Children can tell the difference.

Level 2: Reflecting Accurately

Summarize accurately what your child says (Linehan 1997). This is a wonderful way to validate your child. If your daughter tells you that she feels as if this were the worst day she has ever had and that she wants to stay in her room for the rest of the year, it would be validating to respond, "I can see that you have had a really bad day and that you want to retreat to your room for a very long time." She knows you heard her and aren't trying to argue with her, and she feels that you are showing interest. It's so simple in theory but, again, very hard to enact. Parents want to fix the sadness, but sometimes it's not the right time to try. Usually kids just want to vent their feelings and then move on. Validating your child's feelings will allow her to do this.

Acknowledging feelings and thoughts can be a simple process. Stating that you understand that Phillip is scared, angry, hurt, or whatever he feels may be a form of validation, even if he has just stated his feelings in the same way. Recall a time when you asked someone how some clothing looked on you. You thought your look was flattering, but we all know that our view of the world can be skewed sometimes. How many times have you bought clothes that you loved in the store, only to wonder later what on earth you were thinking? So you look for confirmation. You ask because sometimes it's hard to be sure or to know until someone else validates your feeling. Children sometimes need confirmation about their internal experience, because they are still learning and all of us have times when we are unsure of ourselves.

Another example is when David says he is angry that his friend, James, played with Zachary today instead of him. This isn't the time to give David a lesson by explaining to him that people have more than one friend or that if he shared his toys more with James, James might like him better. Nor is it the time to say that you will call James's mother. Just addressing David's anger in a validating way is all David needs. You cannot fix his feelings about James and Zachary, but you can provide a safe container for your child to share how he feels, and you can validate his feelings.

The first step is to say, "I can see how angry you are." Let him express his feelings and have them acknowledged. Then you can help him learn about multiple friendships or solve problems concerning his friendship skills. He will be better able to listen after he has been heard.

Acknowledging actions is also important. If Danny cleaned up after dinner, then acknowledging that he was helpful and did a good job validates him and also reinforces his good behavior. Recognition in the form of attention and praise for accomplishments, contributions, and effort is validating if it is genuine and deserved.

Your actions can be validating as well. When your child is cold so you hand her a jacket, or when you offer a snack after she comes off the soccer field, because you know she is probably hungry, that is a validating action. Such actions say that you understand her experience and care about her desires.

Children, and sometimes adults, may not always know what they are feeling. Some emotional experiences are easily confused, like excitement and nervousness. Helping children label their feelings accurately is a form of validation. This does not mean telling your child what he is feeling when he says he feels something different. If he is unsure, offer choices or guesses: "So you feel betrayed?" "Do you feel scared?" The ability to label a feeling enhances a person's sense of being in control and gives him more of an idea of what needs to be done. Knowledge is power, and when you know how you feel, you are more in control over what you do next. It's also helpful to know what the primary feeling is. For instance, if your child has invited a friend over to play and the friend declines to come, your child may first feel sad but then start to focus on being angry that the friend didn't want to come. If your child focuses on anger, then he never actually learns to tolerate sadness and also never learns to feel sadness and let it pass. Helping your child learn to identify his primary feeling is extremely important.

Sometimes it's helpful to know what emotions feel like in the body so that you can identify them. Labeling emotions correctly is important information for us to have in making decisions and in reacting appropriately. As mentioned earlier, excitement and anxiety are closely related. People who tend to be anxious often confuse the two and react with trepidation when positive events occur. People also confuse excitement with happiness. When this happens, people think there must be thrilling events in their lives for them to be happy.

When physical sensations accompany anger, we often feel hot, tense, or maybe light-headed, and notice a pounding heart. We usually have an urge to go toward whatever is making us angry. Anger serves the purpose of communicating that something needs to change. The physical symptoms of anxiety include palpitations, fluttering in the stomach, a racing heart, and perhaps feelings of dizziness. We usually have an urge to avoid whatever is creating the anxiety. Helping your child distinguish and identify what they feel can be validating

Level 3: Reading Minds

Mind reading is the third level of validation identified by Linehan (1997). The key here is to make sure you frame your suggestion as a guess. Sometimes just guessing about the feelings or thoughts your child is having can be validating. If your child looks and acts angry, it can be validating to ask if her feelings actually match her expression and behavior. As a parent, you can describe without judgment what you see your child expressing through her face and behavior and ask if that's how she feels. Sometimes you may be surprised! This level of validation may help your child possibly identify more precisely what she feels. Be careful not to assume or imply that your view is accurate. This is speculation on your part that your child has to confirm. Sad and depressed could also be tired and hungry, so you can't always know by observed behavior. This level can help children identify what they feel. It's helpful to remember that children are still learning how to label their internal experiences.

Level 4: Validating Your Child's Behavior in Light of Causes, Like Past Events

Linehan's fourth level of validation (1997) is an important addition. Sometimes behavior is understandable and normal only when we consider what happened in the past. A child who screams at the sight of a bird may look illogical unless you know that he was attacked by a bird a few months ago. Once you consider that past event, his present behavior makes perfect sense.

Level 5: Validating Your Child's Behavior in Light of Present Events and Normal Reactions

Linehan (1997) sees this level as important to helping people know what is normal. We've all wondered at some point or another if we were normal. This level of validation is about giving children feedback about normal responses. To be sad when a pet dies is normal. To be angry when a friend tears up a cherished belonging, to be angry or sad when you are grounded, and to be scared when you are taking a very difficult test are all normal emotions. It's probably not normal to be thrilled when a plane crashes or to be happy that your pet got run over by a car. Talking about true feelings will help to validate them. Your child may be thrilled about the plane crash, because the idea of an exploding plane seems cool to her. She has seen one too many action movies and associates this event with destroying the bad guy. Teaching her about the consequences of a plane crash is validating.

Level 6: Practicing Radical Genuineness by Discussing the Real Stuff

Linehan (1997) uses this level to address the importance of authenticity in an interaction. Psychologists say no one can ever know exactly how someone else feels, which is true. But sometimes, we've had experiences in which we felt as if we knew exactly how someone else felt. We've been there. We know exactly how it feels to lose a parent. We know what it's like to be teased about our appearance. The sixth level of validation is letting yourself be vulnerable with your child by sharing the truth even when it is unpleasant.

Allowing yourself to be vulnerable enables you to talk about truths and experiences that are difficult to discuss. That means being willing to talk about issues your child faces that you probably wish he didn't have to deal with. Validation is communicating that you understand the world your child lives in. If you have a child who is not athletic, perhaps a boy who is more sensitive and intellectual or who is bullied by his classmates, you may tend to keep telling him to stand up for himself and put him on a soccer team so he can make friends. You may tell him that he just has to work to make friends. In truth, some children are not as popular as others, and believe it or not, many of these children don't care. Also, not all kids value being the smartest in the class. If a girl is a bit nerdy and clumsy for her age, the athletic group may not accept her. In the history of teenagers who have been involved in school shootings, the teenagers were consistently teased and felt they did not fit in (Leary et al. 2003). The shootings were about their anger, a need for revenge, and a sense of entitlement, as well as a need for attention. Some studies have suggested that children who are teased may develop post-traumatic stress disorder and act out of trauma. While people do not want to see their children as having difficulty making friends, it's important to recognize and validate this if that's the case. If children feel understood, then at least they can feel that they are not alone. If you can validate what they are experiencing, then you can also address the issues more realistically.

Talking about the real stuff also means talking about the pressures on the popular and high-achieving students. The stress it takes to maintain their social and academic standing can be very high. Their identities are not fully developed yet and, to them, may depend on their keeping their popularity, athletic status, or academic achievements. Saying "You'll do fine; you always do" only increases the pressure they feel. So discussing the real stuff means really addressing the world children and preteens live in. For preteens who hang out with teenagers, it's about discussing drinking and drugs in a realistic way. In an affluent area in our hometown, it's generally accepted that teenagers drink. While this may not be a positive norm, if you lived in this area and asked a teen whether he was exaggerating when he said, "Everyone is doing it," or if you refused to allow a teen to be around friends who drink, the teen would see you as being of no help at all because you do not understand. In such a case, the teen might be right. If drinking parties among your preteen's teenaged friends are popular and frequent, you need to validate this reality and discuss real strategies for him to deal with this social world.

This applies to sexuality as well. Just telling your child to stick to her values is not as effective when you do not recognize the pressures even middle-school students face. How you talk to your children during their elementary- and middle-school years will prepare them to self-validate as they mature into teenagers. When you validate the fact that your child's older friends are talking about how great sex is and that your child worries that she may not get dates if she isn't willing to be sexually active, you are helping her discuss her concerns honestly. This offers a connection for allowing true communication.

Talking about the real stuff means discussing the pressures that children and preteens experience every day. You may hear about a child who is cheating in class, about a child who is invited to a birthday party, about a child who has more money, or that being good looking draws special attention. If your family has a low income, it may be hard to tell your child that you don't have as much money as other families do. Yet your child will face this reality every day. When he goes to school, the wealthier children will be wearing clothes that your child cannot have. Acknowledging this truth without shaming anyone in the family validates your child. Money does not buy happiness and is not a reflection of a person's integrity, intelligence, or value. To be able to hear this message is important, because your child needs to know that you understand his reality and how hard it is to not have a designer wardrobe. Discussing the hard stuff is uncomfortable, but it it's hard for you to talk about and makes you squirm in your seat, think of how it feels for your child. It's tough, but offering a safe and accepting environment for your child to express himself will make all the difference in the world to him and to your relationship with him.

The Importance of Knowing the Levels of Validation

Sometimes what is a validating comment in one situation could be an invalidating one in a different situation. Linehan (1997) notes that the fourth and fifth levels of validation need to be carefully considered, or they could be invalidating. Consider the following example: Misha, an eleven-year-old, has changed schools many times because her parents have had to move for her father's job. One day Misha comes home from school in tears and tells her mother that a girl has been calling her names and turning her friends against her. Her mother wants to validate Misha's feelings, so she says, "Given everything you have been through with changing schools, I understand why that would be so upsetting to you." Her mother uses the fourth level of validation. The problem is that Misha's reaction is normal. Any child would be upset at losing her friends. To say that Misha's upset is understandable because of her past experiences invalidates the fact that her response is completely normal regardless of how many times she has changed schools. Validating normal responses serves as feedback to the child that her emotional response is one most of us would share. The opposite is also true. If a child's emotional response is only understandable and normal because of a past experience, the child needs this information as well. The careful use of the fourth and fifth levels of validation helps the child develop an accurate understanding of her internal experience, which will also help the child cultivate appropriate coping skills.

Exercise 6.1 Practice Recognizing the Levels of Validation

In this exercise, we describe selected situations, for some of which you are asked to identify the level of validation and write a validating statement that fits that level, and for others of which you are given a validating statement or action and asked to identify its level of validation.

1. When Maria was six, a dog bit her mother. Maria saw the wound and went to the doctor with her mother. Now she is eleven, and today is the first day of her school year. A new classmate walks in with a seizure-response dog that goes to school with her. When Maria sees the dog enter the room, she is paralyzed with fear.

   What level of validation best fits this situation?

Write a validating response that fits that level:

2. When Tran was five, the police burst through his door with weapons drawn and arrested his father. The arrest was a mistake, and his father was soon released. Now eight years old, Tran wants a video-game system so he can play violent video games. He sits down on the floor of the store, begging for the console.

    What level of validation is most indicated in this situation?

    Write a validating response that fits that level:

3. Ten-year-old Jenny is furious because her best friend won a singing contest but she herself didn't place in the top three. She tells her mother that it wasn't fair because she knows she can sing better than her friend. Jenny is an exceptionally talented singer, and her mother is confused as to why she didn't win. Her mother responds, "Sometimes we don't understand why someone else wins a contest. When that happens, it hurts and makes us angry. When we feel cheated out of something that's important to us, it's an awful feeling."

    What level of validation did Jenny's mother use?

4. Nine-year-old Crew comes home from school and goes straight to his room, which is unusual behavior for him. Concerned, his mother follows him and finds him lying face down on his bed, obviously fighting tears. She asks questions, but he doesn't respond. His mother says, "I'm guessing that you're really upset about something that happened today at school, so upset that it's hard to talk about it."

What level of validation did Crew's mother use?

5. Twelve-year-old Cecilia just learned a difficult dance move in tap-dancing class. Her mother goes to the class to watch her; she sits on the side and keeps her attention on Cecilia's dance.

   What level of validation did Cecilia's mother use?

6. Eleven-year-old Sadie tells her parents that the teacher canceled the test that was originally scheduled for the next day. She wants to go to a friend's house since she doesn't have to study. Her father says, "I really want to believe you, and you may very well be telling me the truth. The problem is that over the past couple of months, you've not been truthful about your homework, so I have doubts now that you're telling me the truth."

   What level of validation did Sadie's father use?

ANSWERS:

1. *Level 4:* validating in light of past events. Most children would not react so negatively to a calm dog in a safe situation, plus there's a reason in Maria's past for her to be so scared. Any statement that says that Maria's fear is understandable because of her past would be a level 4 response, such as "It's completely understandable that you were so scared today because of the time that dog bit your mother."

2. *Level 2:* reflecting accurately. "You want that game system so badly that it seems like you won't be able to stand it if you don't get it."

3. *Level 2:* reflecting accurately. Reflect feelings. The mother restates what she heard Jenny say. She doesn't make excuses or upset Jenny more by blaming the judges.

4. *Level 3:* reading minds. Crew does not tell his mother how he feels, so she has to guess. She doesn't demand to know what trouble he got into or what his grade was on the test he took that day. Her first priority is validating his feelings. When he is better able or more willing to talk, she may learn that he is more upset that he will be grounded than he is about the bad grade. She can validate those feelings too, but he will still be grounded.

5. *Level 1:* showing interest and being present. The mother is fully present and showing interest. She does not offer a critique.

6. *Level 6:* discussing the real stuff. The father is being open and honest about his thoughts without judging his daughter.

Wrapping Up

This chapter has been about learning the specific levels of validation and how to apply them. You have learned that in certain parenting situations, one level of validation may be indicated over others, but in many cases you can choose more than one of the many levels. Validating parenting means that you are present in each interaction with your child, which better equips you to be attuned to which level of validation is most appropriate in a given situation. Remember, like any new skill, validating parenting takes practice, and the practice is worth it. We believe that your relationship with your child will only improve when you practice your validation skills. In the next chapter, we'll look more in depth at how to practice validating parenting.

Chapter 7

How to Apply the Levels of Validation to Validating Parenting

As with learning any new behavior, you must practice validation until it becomes a natural part of your parenting. Sometimes parents get discouraged when they can't make changes right away. Change is a process. In the interest of helping you be as successful as possible, we'll first discuss the process of change and how it works. Then we'll focus on exercises involving the levels of validation you learned in the last chapter. Note that we've renamed some the levels identified by Marsha Linehan.

The Process of Change: You Can Do It

Parents who learn about validation often find it difficult to put into practice. We think you would agree that changing your behavior is difficult even when it makes sense to do so. Changing how you communicate with your child will mean making a commitment to the new behavior and practicing the new skill repeatedly. Change usually happens not all at once, but in steps. Part of the process is accepting that a new skill takes practice to master and that you will not remember to use the new skill consistently for some time. Be patient with yourself and remember to keep your emotions in check as you are learning. It can be frustrating, but perseverance will pay off. Also, as mentioned earlier, you will see such a remarkable response in your child that you will be validated and motivated to continue!

There are six stages to how people change (Prochaska, Norcross, and DiClemente 1994). In the first stage, *precontemplation*, there is no intention to change in the foreseeable future. This may mean that there's no recognition that change is needed, but not necessarily. It may mean that you know that change is important but have no wish to make the change. In the second stage, *contemplation*, there is an awareness of the need for change and serious thought is being given to addressing the problem, but no action is being taken and there's no commitment to making any changes. In the third stage, *preparation*, there is intention and commitment to take action within a short period of time, such as a month. In the fourth stage, *action*, there is change in behavior, experiences, or environment to address the problem. This requires considerable time and energy, and a strong commitment. During the fifth stage, *maintenance*, people work to prevent relapsing into old ways and to strengthen the changes and progress they've made.

So the first step is to look at your commitment to changing your communication style with your child. Maybe this isn't the right time. Maybe you want to change but have no extra energy right now. Maybe you aren't convinced it's important. If that's the case, then wait—no problem. Maybe spend some time thinking about what you've read. What we don't want you to do is make a halfhearted decision to work on validating parenting, without truly working on it, and then toss the book aside, claiming that it didn't work. So if you are ready to commit and to infuse that commitment with energy and accountability, then read on.

Setting Realistic Goals

Part of enacting successful change is setting realistic goals. If you have been reacting impulsively to emotions most of your life, you will not change that in one week, two weeks, or even three months. Set small, achievable goals and build on your progress, and you will see significant gains that will encourage you to reach your long-term goal. Take each step we outline in this chapter and practice it until you feel comfortable that you have mastered it. Then move on to the next step.

One way to set good goals is by using SMART (Doran 1981), which stands for *specific*, observable behaviors that are *measurable, attainable, realistic*, and *time limited*. This means you know exactly what you want to achieve and have a way of measuring it. Your goal is attainable (you aren't trying to turn your blood orange) and realistic (you aren't trying to grow twelve inches in one week). An example of such a goal would be to exercise for ten minutes five times a week, or to practice being present three times in the next week. As mentioned in chapter 6, learning the skill of being present with your child takes practice. It's not parents' natural inclination to be present with their children while doing the dishes, cooking dinner, walking the dog, changing the baby's diaper, or driving the carpool. Being present can be the last thing parents think about. So in addition to your motivation and commitment, you'll also need a reminder to practice and a way of measuring your specific, observable behavior. You might want to keep a chart, have an accountability partner, and put a reminder in your phone calendar. We know you can do it.

Tracking Your Progress

This is so important that we want to say it again. Having accountability and measuring your progress are crucial parts of learning a new skill. We suggest that you record your practice with each step in learning how to validate. Writing down what you did and reviewing the results makes a difference. After you practice each level of validation, we suggest continuing to record your success in a journal. Later in this chapter, you'll find exercises for practicing the levels of validation.

Practicing the Levels of Validation

So you've made a commitment, you understand the importance of applying validating parenting, and you're ready to practice. Let's start with level 1, being present and showing interest. First we'll review the concept and offer some examples, and then we'll suggest some steps to follow. Finally we'll ask you to practice.

Level 1: Being Present and Showing Interest

Remember, being present means that you are fully aware of your interaction with your child and not distracted by other thoughts or activities. You can't always be fully present when you are with your child, but sometimes you can intentionally make a point to validate your child's existence and importance by focusing wholly on him rather than thinking of the tasks you have to do. Being present means that while you are with your child, you are not thinking about work or about how stupid it is for you to be upset about something your boss said. It means you are willing to take the time to just listen to and be with your child.

You can often just be present when there is nothing else you can do. A situation in which it's validating for you to just be there for your child might be when your child has to endure a painful medical procedure or when there's a hurricane warning. This would mean accepting that your child is scared and that there's nothing you can do. When your child's best friend moves away, or your child loses a school election or doesn't get into the college she desperately wanted to attend, this is a situation in which there is little to be said. Just being there is all your child needs for you to validate her.

Being reassuring at such moments can be more upsetting than helpful. Telling your child that the family pet who died is in heaven or that there's nothing to worry about, even though the winds are howling outside, doesn't seem right even to young children. They are sad and scared, and you may be telling them there's no reason to feel that way. Being present is letting children have their feelings rather than pretending that there's no reason to have them.

These types of situations don't happen daily. While these situations are best met with this first level of validation, being present can also be validating in most other types of situations. Children can sense whenever you are fully present, and the 100 percent interest and attention feels very supportive. You can practice this level of validation in almost any situation. Watching your child swing, drawing with your child, reading to your child, or engaging in any interaction by being fully present says to your child that he is important to you. For older children, you might watch them dance or listen to a song they particularly like. Even playing a video game with your child on your cell phone can be a way to practice being present.

Being fully present requires energy and the willingness to connect in an intimate way. Sometimes people are more comfortable with distance and distractions that decrease the intensity of being present with someone. When you try being fully present, with no other thoughts in your head, notice your comfort level. If you don't feel at ease, consider why that might be and solve the problem if you can. If you can't, then, often, simply practicing despite your discomfort helps.

STEPS FOR BEING PRESENT

1. Give your child your attention. Let go of distractions in your mind or the environment.

2. Focus on your child's experience, not yours. Get out of your head. Notice your child's reactions and expressions. If you have thoughts like *How am I doing?* let them go and refocus on your child.

3. The child leads the experience, not you. What's interesting to children is not always interesting to parents. Sometimes parents think they can make the activity better or more fun for children, but the minute you take over the activity, you've essentially told the child that you can do it better. Children often don't consider the age and experience issue, but rather see themselves as not good enough. This isn't a message you want to give your children. So when being present with your child, be a follower. Watch what your child does, and let that be enough.

4. Try to repeat your child's words in your responses to her. This guideline is similar to not leading the experience. Sometimes by your words, you can change an experience your child is having into something different. Be careful not to interpret your child's pretend game or art as something other than what she created.

Logan, aged eight, has toy soldiers set up behind the couch in the living room. His mother sits beside him and watches him play. Logan explains that the green soldiers are fighting the brown soldiers, because the green soldiers stole money from the brown ones. Logan's mother doesn't say, "Why not have them fight to protect their country?" She just watches. Soon Logan is telling her how to move the brown soldiers. Logan's mother asks questions about how he wants to play the game but doesn't try to change what he wants to do.

For one week, practice being present with your child. Choose a period of time and start with a few minutes, maybe five or ten. Join your child in whatever she is doing and observe. Respond to her questions or requests, but don't make any suggestions. If your mind wanders away from what you are doing with your child, gently and nonjudgmentally bring it back. It is almost certain that your mind will wander; that's normal. Listen to a song your child likes, watch a trick she taught the dog, or listen to what she did at a friend's house. Remember to keep your expectations for yourself realistic. Plan to be intentional about it. This experience won't naturally happen.

An example that would require more time would be moving furniture in your daughter's room. Your daughter wants to rearrange her room in a way that makes sense to her. Find a time when you can do this with her without worrying or thinking about anything but her and the room. If you can find this time, let her lead the process. Ask her where she wants her bed, and put it there, even if you don't agree. If you can successfully navigate this process, you will be present without judgment for your daughter, which will mean the world to her, more than if you hired a decorator and had a famous designer hand-select all the fabric.

Be careful about getting impatient, trying to help, or suggesting changes. For example, Justin comes home from first grade excited about showing his dad how to make a Jacob's ladder with string. He gets confused and has difficulty getting the ladder to work, and his dad reaches for the string: "Let me show you how." Justin says, "No," and runs away. Justin's dad probably means well, but it will be more validating to let Justin struggle until he can do it or get help from someone else, then come back to show his dad. Justin's dad could ask, "Do you want me to help?" giving Justin the choice. Being present means setting aside your own agenda. Justin's dad wants him to be successful, so he tries to help, which takes away Justin's experience of his dad's being present with him. Instead, his dad becomes a teacher and a helper.

Amy colors a picture of a banana and runs to show it to her mother, who comments: "Amy, you know bananas are yellow." It would be validating by showing interest to say, "Well, that's a beautiful red banana. Why did you choose red?" Amy says she wanted to color the banana red because she likes red best.

Following a child's lead means that sometimes, in appropriate circumstances, like on the playground or in a pretend game, the child gets to be in charge. By being in charge, he gets to be in control. Since children are powerless most of the time (being told when to eat, go to the bathroom, go to bed, and so on), it's novel for them to be in charge. It's validating to the child that others can accept his ideas and sometimes let him lead.

Showing interest in what your child is doing and feeling is validating. When someone shows genuine interest in what's important to you, whether it's cooking, sports, politics, crafts, volunteering, conservation, or whatever is dear to your heart, think about your reaction. For many people, it brings about a feeling of camaraderie and a sense of being alike, or fitting together. Sharing your interests with others with whom you have a bond strengthens that bond.

STEPS FOR SHOWING INTEREST

1. Observe your child to see what is interesting to her in the moment. Children's interests change quickly sometimes, but that doesn't make their interests less important.

2. When you notice your child showing interest, make a comment reflecting your understanding of his interest: "Hey, you are spending a lot of time coloring today." Questions such as "Why do you like that?" may be ones that younger children cannot answer. Comments present less pressure for children than questions and are seen more as initiating statements. Remember to be nonjudgmental in your comments, which means that you do not appraise your child's activity either positively or negatively.

3. If it's feasible, try the activity yourself. Share what the experience was like for you. If you aren't as good as your child at the activity, this would be a good opportunity for your child to teach you something that she knows. Often computer games and computers are an area where this is easily practiced.

Acknowledging actions is a way of showing interest. It's another way of saying to your child that you are paying attention and that he is an important member of the family. Noting that he was dressed on time for school, helped a sibling in some way, reached out to a friend, or did his homework without being asked is an example. Noticing positive actions helps your child see that you notice more than just the behaviors that annoy you! You happen to notice that your twelve-year-old son spent the entire afternoon teaching his six-year-old cousin how to ride her bike. You describe to him how you watched him thoughtfully teach little Susie how to ride her bike and how much you appreciate his taking time with her. You may even point out that many people before him tried unsuccessfully to teach her and that you are pleased at his ability to take the time to show her. It's only a short bunch of words, but merely observing and pointing out positive behavior will mean the world to your child.

Acknowledging actions goes beyond noticing positive behaviors, though. It also means noticing a change in behavior. If your child is usually bouncy and energetic but, one evening, is quiet and lacks energy, acknowledging the change in her actions would be validating. A validating parent would say, "I notice that you seem to be less energetic than you usually are." There may or may not be something wrong with your child, but if there is, this is likely to open the door for her to talk with you about it. Remember now, as always, to avoid judgment.

Exercise 7.1 Practice Being Present and Showing Interest

Practice once a day for a week and record your experiences in your notebook. Notice if being present gets easier or harder. What judgments do you make? Do you tell yourself you don't have time for this? Do you think *This is silly*? Plan to record the day and time, the activity your child is doing, how difficult it is for you to stay present, and any reactions you or your child has to the experience. The headings might look as follows:

Day and time:

Activity:

How difficult was it to stay present and show interest (on a scale of 1 to 10, with 10 being very difficult)?

Judgments I noticed myself making about myself:

Judgments I noticed myself making about my child:

Outcome of practicing being present and showing interest:

What got in my way?

What I want to do differently next time:

Level 2: Validating Listening

Validating listening, the level that Marsha Linehan calls "reflective listening," means that you listen carefully and restate in a genuine way what your child has said to you. Level 2 incorporates level 1 in that you have to be present to be a validating listener. To practice, choose a time each day when you will do nothing other than listen to what your child has to say. This means no activities other than focusing on your child. Summarize or restate to your child what he has said to you in a way that shows that you are listening and interested. Do this as naturally as possible. Often, when parents listen to their children, they want to offer solutions or ways to fix their children's problems. This is not validating listening. Parents also may rush their children so that they can get to the eleven other things they need to do at that moment. Don't practice validating listening if you don't have the time to commit to it. It does take time but not as much as you might think.

Level 3: Guessing about Feelings

Listen carefully, as you did when practicing level 2 validation. Listen for feelings or thoughts your child may not be expressing directly. In a caring manner, guess what your child might be thinking or feeling, and check it out with him. If your child disagrees with your guess, don't argue, even if you are pretty sure that you are right. Ask for clarification.

Think about this example of acknowledging feelings: Eight-year-old Lilly loves one-on-one attention. When she is having a good time with someone, it's difficult for her to stop when it's time for the person to leave. Whenever her grandmother comes to visit, she focuses all of her attention on Lilly, playing dress-up and participating in whatever activity Lilly desires. When her grandmother has to leave, Lilly goes into emotional overload, expressed by crying or saying no repeatedly. The most recent time her grandmother left, Lilly kicked and hit her mother and grandmother. Lilly's mother validated that it was hard to say good-bye, but she was also firm that it was not okay to hit. After her mother guessed her feelings, Lilly was able to say that she was upset because she didn't like for her grandmother to leave when she was having a good time. Being able to say that she didn't want the fun to end helped her to manage her behavior differently. If her mother had just reprimanded her and not recognized the feeling, Lilly could well have learned that she was bad to feel so upset, which might result in her feeling angry at herself. This would only increase the likelihood that the next good-bye would be difficult, creating a negative spiral.

Level 4: Validating in Light of Past Experiences

Validating in light of past experiences is about recognizing that sometimes a child's reactions are more about what happened in the past than what's happening in the present. Acknowledging that your child's reaction is understandable due to his past experience gives him truth. A child who broke his leg skiing may be afraid to go skiing again. A child who has moved many times and has to say good-bye once more, to a friend who is moving, may be more upset than a child who hasn't had that experience. On the other hand, a child with that experience may be accustomed to saying good-bye and react better than most children. The idea is to help your child understand that his actions, feelings, and thoughts are normal in the context of his past experience.

What experiences in your child's past are likely to affect her emotional responses, thinking, or behavior in the present? In what ways do you see these past experiences affecting your child's emotional responses, thinking, or behavior in the present? The next time you notice these behaviors, validate your child's feelings, thoughts, and behaviors in terms of the past. Pay attention to your child's reaction.

Level 5: Validating in Light of What Is Normal

Validating normal thoughts, feelings, actions, and sensations is about helping your child know that he is normal. People aren't born knowing whether their internal experience is normal or how other people feel. Doesn't everyone at times feel left out, ashamed, or inadequate? Understanding that your reactions are normal helps you to accept them. Opportunities to validate normal thoughts, feelings, behaviors, and sensations happen every day. When your child expresses frustration about having to go to bed or not getting to play with a friend, that's an opportunity to validate normal feelings. For many reasons, parents sometimes don't want to validate normal feelings. Validating feelings as normal means that you have to acknowledge that your child has certain feelings. An adoptive child's statement that he misses his biological mother may tear the adoptive mother's heart in two such that she fears any discussion of this subject. If your child laments not having cake because she is gluten intolerant, let her feel sad. Don't lie and tell her the cupcake was gross. In truth, validating your child's thoughts and feelings may defuse his desires and the intensity of the feeling.

Start now, for at least three times a day for two weeks, to validate your child as having normal reactions, thoughts, and feelings. Note the validations you give each day. The idea is to increase your awareness and to make validation a natural part of your parenting. At the end of the two weeks, just keep track each day of how you validated your child.

Level 6: Being Genuine, or Discussing the Real Stuff

To talk about the real issues in your child's life, you obviously have to know what the real stuff is. How do you find that out? One way is to simply ask your child. Another way is to pay attention to the issues that are happening in the classroom. When another child is disciplined for fighting at school, it may seem to be none of your business if your child was not involved. But perhaps that fight was the result of bullying or teasing, which means that these difficulties may be the real stuff you need to discuss with your child because that's happening in her world. Another way to know the real issues is to talk with other parents. They may know about problems that you don't know about. If it's happening to other children in your school, your child is exposed, even if it's only through talk.

Pay attention to memos and alerts, for not just the precautions to take but also the subject matter. If an alert is issued, it's a concern your child has been exposed to and may need help understanding and coping with. Weather warnings, such as hurricanes, floods, tornadoes, thunderstorms, and other acts of nature, such as fires, are a sign to you that your child may need to talk. Pay attention to comments or requests that seem to come from nowhere. "Mom, can I get a nose job?" may be due to peer pressure, but it could also be due to peer rejection or taunting.

Remember that whatever's happening in your home is also important to discuss. It's important to validate your children's concerns. If you and your spouse are not getting along, you probably don't want to discuss it with your children and may believe that it's inappropriate to discuss with them. However, the tension and arguments do not go unnoticed. While you do not need to give adult information to children or unnecessarily frighten them, validating that you are arguing more lately is helpful to the children.

If you are sure that there will be no divorce in the reasonable future, then you can assure your children of that fact. Children are aware of divorce from television and school. They do not know which marital arguments are threatening. To young children, any argument could mean that their parents are getting divorced. Validating any thoughts and fears they may have and answering whatever questions they have is important, as long as it does not involve private information.

If someone in the family is ill or dies, talking about that person with the children is important. In our practice, we have seen adults who, as children, lost a sibling and had no idea what happened until they grew up. When Jeff was ten, his sister was removed from the home; one day, when he came home from school, his sister was gone. His parents never spoke of her or explained where she went. It wasn't until Jeff was older that he learned that she was placed in an institution. Think of the fear he lived with for many years. Had his parents explained what was happening and talked about the real stuff, Jeff may not have needed to numb himself when he became a teenager.

Talking about the real stuff means being honest about social situations. Sometimes parents want to protect children from the harsh reality of acceptance and rejection, but children experience it every day. If parents ignore it, children may believe it doesn't happen to adults, only to them.

The truth is, not everyone will like your child. Teaching a child that not everyone in the world will like her is a tremendous lesson to teach. Of course, as a parent, you want everyone to love your children, but really you know that it doesn't work that way. Think about your own experiences in life. Not everyone likes you. It isn't the end of the world. Yet for kids, it may feel that way. Validating the feeling will help.

PHYSICAL BOUNDARIES

Validation is about not only dealing with feelings and thoughts but also recognizing your child's comfort with his own body. At any age, if your child does not want to change clothes in front of another adult, validating his sense of privacy is important. If your daughter doesn't want her father supervising her bath, respect that need for privacy. Recognizing and validating her own-ership of her own body is part of preparing her to be able to have respect for her boundaries in later years, when there are many pressures to ignore this sense. If your child knows that her opinions count and that her sense of pri-vacy and ownership of her body is valid, this can only help in encounters with people who exploit children's boundaries and with other children who may not have appropriate boundaries.

While at school, a five-year-old boy asked to see ten-year-old Mattie's breasts. Mattie, whose parents consistently validated her right to privacy and her physical boundaries, was scared by the younger child's request. She then told both her teacher and her mother. When Mattie reaches age sixteen, she will quite likely have the same ability to set her boundaries. Imagine if Mattie couldn't set her own physical boundaries. She might be vulnerable to comply-ing with the request, which might have been damaging to both children.

Exercise 7.2 Practice Discussing the Real Issues

Discussing the real stuff may be one of the more challenging levels of validation. If you find yourself giving excuses for why you do not need to do this with your child, then maybe the idea is making you uncom-fortable. This exercise may help you identify the reasons for your dis-comfort and help you overcome it. Answer the following questions:

What issues do you know you need to discuss with your child?

What blocks you from discussing these concerns?

How can you overcome the roadblocks?

What can you tell your child that will help him deal with these issues? Remember to consider his perspective.

After you've talked about one of the real issues with your child, what did you learn that you will do differently next time?

Wrapping Up

This chapter has been about practicing. To learn a new skill, practice is critical. We hope that your practice with your children has been a positive experience, and we urge you to continue to review and practice the levels of validation until they become a natural part of your parenting. Doing so will offer many benefits to both you and your child. In the next chapter, we'll look at what could get in the way of your using validating parenting.

Chapter 8

Dealing with Roadblocks to Your Success

Sometimes it's helpful to troubleshoot your plans to see what could get in the way of your success with validating parenting. After you have identified potential roadblocks, you will then make a plan for dealing with those issues.

Best Intentions

One possible roadblock is your wish, as a parent, to raise responsible children. Parents can inadvertently invalidate their children out of a sincere and well-intentioned desire to treat their kids "right." Parents who are involved and engaged with their children and aware of their children's reactions, moods, and lives are invested in their children's success, happiness, morality, and friendships. This could result in parents' working to eradicate behaviors and statements that resemble selfishness, lack of appreciation, entitlement, or pride. Such parents are guiding their children and working hard at raising them. Unfortunately, by doing so in an invalidating manner, they risk creating the very issues they are concerned about, such as a poor sense of self, lack of confidence in decision-making ability, lack of identity, poor self-esteem, and many problems that arise from invalidation. To suggest that such parents do not want the best for their children makes no sense at all. But sometimes their desire for their children's success becomes the very roadblock they are trying to prevent. Most parents have had the experience of invalidating their children in an attempt to guide them, so be careful. Don't let your desire for their success drive you to invalidate them. Have you ever seen the TV show *Toddlers and Tiaras*? Many of the moms want their little girls to be beauty queens, but many of the little girls don't want that. By "doing everything right" and putting their children in beauty pageants, these parents are invalidating their children's desire not to participate.

Your Own Emotions

To validate effectively, you must be able to manage your own emotions. When you are upset, you are more likely to say things you do not mean. Children can be provocative and often know how to push your buttons. Some parents get caught up in the emotion and can't distinguish the emotion from reality. It's as if the emotion becomes so large that reality is thrown out the window. Remember, you are separate from your feelings, but your feelings are valid. Being able to notice that you have feelings differs from *being* your feeling.

Noticing your own internal experience is part of being emotionally healthy. This means that you are aware of your own body-and-mind experiences. Noticing that your body is tense or that your pulse has quickened is part of being able to manage your emotions. Being aware of what you are experiencing means you are taking the first step to being able to manage your actions. When you are aware of your body sensations, you will be aware of any urges you have to take action. It may be that you have the urge to yell, to throw something, or to hit the wall. This is an urge, and, often, when you act on urges that are tied to intense emotional reactions, you will regret the action later. Noticing the urge and substituting a more constructive behavior until you can calm down and think without intense emotion will allow you to avoid invalidating your child. Gradually the ability to take a break, to exercise, or to just breathe until you are calmer becomes more natural and easier to do.

To be able to effectively validate your child, you need to be able to react nonjudgmentally and stay calm. It's very hard to validate anyone when you are angry or scared. This means that having the skill of managing your own emotions is essential to validation. When you are upset emotionally, you need to learn to take a step back and distance yourself until you are calm enough to truly consider what is important in the situation and what message you want to give your child. There is no urgency in most situations, even though your emotions sometimes make you feel as if the situation is urgent. So let some time pass. Then you may be able to recognize that your child was excited that her friend was coming to visit and ran to the door out of excitement. You may also be able to validate that she genuinely felt bad about breaking the vase. She still broke a rule and didn't think about the possible consequences of her decision, but perhaps you will be able to stop yourself from telling her that she is a selfish kid who never thinks. The ability to discuss the facts of the situation will help you be much more effective in your communication.

Remembering that your goal is to help your child grow to be an independent, confident child who trusts his values and decisions will help you to manage the daily frustrations of dealing with your son, who repeatedly leaves food to spoil in his room along with smelly soccer clothes. Yelling at him, telling him he is irresponsible, or complaining will not help you reach your goal. Although it may feel like the thing to do at the time, that's not one of the steps to raising a validated child!

Accepting Your Child's Less-than-Stellar Qualities

Garrison Keillor describes Lake Wobegon as a place where all children are above average. That brings a smile to most of us, as we recognize that we tend to believe that our children are above average, outstanding even. Think specifically about one of your children, maybe the one who is more difficult for you. Consider all of her positive qualities, qualities that you enjoy. Now think about the qualities that are more difficult to accept; perhaps she shares a quality with you that you don't like in yourself. Maybe she procrastinates, is shy, is lazy, or tends to be easily upset. Most likely, when you consider those qualities, you are thinking about how to change them and are seeing them as undesirable. The truth is those characteristics are part of who your child is. If you look at them as something you need to change, you probably react negatively whenever you observe them. For example, if you wish that your daughter were more social, you may get upset when she chooses to spend time by herself rather than play with a classmate who lives nearby. Despite your good intention to help her become more social, you may very well invalidate her. If you want her to develop better social skills, making a plan to do that will be more helpful than letting your anger or disapproval of her current social self push her.

Lose the Judgment

Stealing is wrong, and so is cheating. But the child doing the stealing or cheating isn't wrong. If that were true, every one of us would be in big trouble, because we've all done regrettable things that weren't the right choices. The problem is that when a child does something wrong, such as disregarding the rules, stealing, or lying, parents may judge him in some way. Children make mistakes. Isn't that part of what growing up is about? Parents think that judging, or maybe withdrawing love, is part of teaching their children right from wrong. The truth is that disappointment in behavior and consequences is part of teaching right and wrong behavior, whereas withdrawing love and judging teach that the *child* is wrong. The latter is very different and harmful.

The following exercise will help you accept your child's less-desirable qualities.

Exercise 8.1 Practice Accepting Your Child's Less-than-Stellar Qualities

1. List the qualities that you find less desirable in your child.

2. Do you understand why you consider those qualities to be a problem?

3. Is there a positive side to those qualities?

4. If you accepted these qualities, what would happen?

5. If you don't accept these qualities, what will happen?

6. If you don't accept these qualities, how will it affect your child?

7. How will it affect you to accept them?

8. Can you see the difference between accepting and agreeing?

All Work and No Fun

In this busy world of ours, your awareness of having a fabulous family may take a back seat to the stress of being unable to get everything done or the exhaustion you feel from a fast-paced life. Sometimes our children become tasks on a long to-do list, and we forget to enjoy them as people. Taking time to do things you really enjoy doing with your child will help you manage your emotions better when you are upset or frustrated. Really enjoying your relationship with your child will make validating her easier.

This doesn't mean just doing something that your children love to do, but doing something that both they and you enjoy. If you can't think of anything that you enjoy doing with them, then that's an important issue to address. Family relationships are stronger when parents and children have positive experiences together.

The negative aspects of parenting, such as seeing shoes and clothes strewn on the floor, are also part of the dream you had of being a parent. View these situations as reminders of how grateful you are to have your family. When you see food on the floor under the table and candy wrappers hidden under the bed, let those be reminders of how lucky you are to have such a wonderful family and how much you wanted these children. That doesn't mean you won't address the candy wrappers or other issues, but if you can look at them as reminders of what you are grateful for, what you wished for, then you may be able to handle these issues without invalidating your children.

Parental Shame

Shame is about feeling that you're not good enough. When you don't feel you're good enough, it's difficult to validate your child. When something triggers your shame, you may invalidate your child out of your own discomfort.

Many parents feel shame about their parenting, often believing that they are not good enough as parents. They compare themselves to other parents, who seem to be superparents. These parents volunteer, have other kids over to their houses, entertain, show up for their children's school activities, and look great while doing it. That negative comparison is one way some parents feel shame, but the reasons for not feeling good enough vary greatly. Mothers feel shame whether they work or stay at home full-time. In difficult economic times, fathers may feel less than adequate, because they are unable to provide for their families. Mothers may worry that they don't cook or help enough with their child's homework.

Shame is about feeling inadequate, not good enough, and like you don't belong. If your child is screaming at you and other parents are watching, you may scream back out of your own shame. When your shame is triggered, a fight-or-flight response is also triggered. The fight part seems to be about the need to blame someone else for the way you feel.

One sure way to increase your shame is to shame yourself, show a lack of self-compassion, or label yourself in a negative way. For example, calling yourself "stupid," "dumb," or "a failure" when you make parenting mistakes will increase your anxiety and lead to your lashing out, blaming, or withdrawing. None of those behaviors is helpful to you or your children. We observe that people who carry a great deal of shame around their parenting often compare their distorted worst to others' perceived best. It also seems that feeling shame as a parent begets shameful parenting behavior, a cycle that begets more shame.

If shame is an issue for you, we encourage you to read Brené Brown's (2007) book *I Thought It Was Just Me (but It Isn't): Telling the Truth about Perfectionism, Inadequacy, and Power*. You might also want to consult a therapist who is familiar with treating shame. Sometimes just discussing it with a professional can be more validating than you could imagine.

Understanding and being aware of your shame-related behavior is the first step in managing it effectively. This doesn't mean you will never again act out of shame. You will, but you will be less likely to do so and more likely to pull out of it when you do. Overcoming shame is about accepting your human-ness and—instead of hiding or blaming—standing up, looking someone in the eye, and speaking out. "Yes, I ate ten doughnuts, and yes, I was late pick-ing up my child from school." "Yes, I work and couldn't attend my child's school play." Hold your head high.

Feeling inadequate is normal. If you can accept that and let go of the drive to be the perfect parent, you will react in more natural ways and be able to validate human fallibility in your children.

Poor Self-Care

Part of being able to manage your emotions is to be sure that you take good care of yourself. Are you taking the medications that you need? Are you see-ing a physician when you need to? Are you getting time for yourself and time for you and your partner? Are you doing activities that you enjoy and eating in healthy ways? It's important to live your life in ways that help you feel more in control of your schedule and activities. When you are in charge of yourself, you are less vulnerable to letting other things control what you say or do. Try to take care of yourself as you would take care of your child. Of course, you must respond to some events immediately, but living with a sense of urgency and feeling controlled by events leaves you feeling drained and frustrated. Whenever you avoid taking action, you feel out of control. For example, if a friend comes over every evening at six for a drink with you when you would prefer to be with your family, but you don't say anything, you will feel irritable and fatigued and be vulnerable to losing control of your feelings. You are avoiding saying something to your friend about your own desires and are not taking care of yourself. You will then be more likely to be irritable with your children.

You can't control some events. For example, perhaps your own parent, who is difficult, needs to stay with you for three weeks due to a medical prob-lem. Your house is small and is up for sale, you have young children, and you aren't getting enough sleep. All of this creates a sense of resentment and the feeling of being out of control. There may be some parts of this experience that you can control. Perhaps you could have your children share a room so that your parent could stay in the guest room rather than your room. And you might decide to avoid having agents show your house during this time. Taking steps to take care of yourself reduces your stress and allows you to be more emotionally healthy for your children. This is easiest to accomplish when you are taking good care of yourself.

Distorted Thinking Affecting Your Actions

A *cognitive distortion* is a belief you hold that has no truth. Albert Ellis spent his life researching people's emotional reactions based on their beliefs and conceived the ABC *theory of emotions* (Ellis and Harper 1975). ABC stands for activating event, beliefs, and consequence. First, there is an activating event. Something happens. You interpret that event based on your beliefs. Then there is a consequence to that belief. For example, suppose the activating event is that your friend has a party. If your belief is that your friend didn't invite you because she's mad at you, then you may call her and tell her how mad you are at her for not being invited. In truth she's not having a party at all. She thought about it and discussed it but never followed through. Your call damaged the relationship and caused you unnecessary upset. Distortions that upset us greatly make our upset seem valid. Saying untrue things to ourselves and convincing ourselves of their truth affects our emotions and behaviors.

Some typical cognitive distortions that lead to invalidation of our children follow.

Overgeneralization

You may think that because a child didn't get a good grade on a paper, he will fail his classes, be lazy about doing any homework, and not learn anything in school. One less-than-desirable grade or even a failing grade may mean many things, including that your child had an off day. We all have off days. Jumping from a single bad grade to the child's failing school is an overgeneralization.

Allowing your child to deal with the consequences of the failing grade without overgeneralizing could offer an opportunity for him to learn about cause and effect and about taking responsibility for his actions. Before you learned the validating parenting concepts, if your child called you because he forgot his homework and he was worried about his grade, you might have said to him, "If you were more responsible, this wouldn't happen. Now I have to interrupt my day just because you never think. You think I have nothing to do? You just never think, do you? Next time, I'll just let you fail." Those statements represent overgeneralization. He does think, and he knows you are busy. As a parent, you think you are teaching and not letting your child get away with irresponsible behavior, but actually you are doing the opposite. You are letting him get away with irresponsible behavior and are invalidating him. Most likely he is thinking about how mean you are or what a lousy person he is, not about how he could do things differently in the future. Overgeneralizing can shut your child down. Rather than overgeneralize, try validation. A validating statement would be "I'm so sorry you forgot your homework. Remember last week, when I said I couldn't bring it to you if this happened again? I have to stick to that." It may seem easier to be mad at your child and still take his homework to him than to bear the discomfort of his getting a zero that you could have prevented.

All-or-Nothing Thinking

This is one of the harder distortions to overcome. It's difficult to not think in black and white when you see no gray, or middle ground, with your child. Your child wins or loses, is wonderful or horrible, depending on the type of situation that happened most recently. This cognitive distortion can lead to a roller coaster of ups and downs, and your child will be anxious and confused and dependent on your evaluation of her that day as to whether or not she is an okay person. For example, your daughter comes home from school and announces that she has been elected to student council. You respond, "I'm so proud of you! You are so popular and have so many friends. That's wonderful." The next day, she comes home and says her best friend has broken off the friendship. You respond, "Did you treat her horribly like you treat me? I know I won't put up with it." This message to your daughter is unclear, as most all-or-nothing thoughts are.

Jumping to Conclusions

When you see your child with money you know he didn't get from you, you may jump to the conclusion that he has stolen the money. Or if you see your child trying to hide something from you, you may assume he is doing something he shouldn't. Perhaps he is hiding a present for you, or maybe he earned some money from his godparents. Parents can also jump to conclusions about grades ("You didn't study") or about the way their children feel about them: "I know you are mad at me," or "You wish Jacob's father were your father." Conclusions like these are usually more about the parent's fears than about what the child thinks. Certainly children get angry and say they hate their parents. That's normal. But children get past being angry and bond with their parents. They don't want to trade you in.

Ignoring or Discounting the Positive

Some parents are quick to point out a child's need to improve but fail to mention the child's positive behaviors and praiseworthy actions. It's as if the positive doesn't merit attention, is expected, or doesn't matter. It's also true that some parents do not give themselves credit for what they do well as parents and pay attention only to the mistakes they think they have made. A parent who does this might argue that the positive doesn't need attention, that only the areas that need improvement require attention. While this may initially sound true, it actually isn't. First of all, to have an accurate picture of yourself, you must include what you do well. Paying attention only to what you don't do well distorts the picture. In addition, paying attention to the positive gives you encouragement to keep working at your goal and helps your overall mood. It also gives you an idea of what works. Remembering the positives will help you stay in balance with the negatives.

Making Assumptions

"I know what you're thinking, and you might as well forget it." This can be so confusing to a child. What if the child is thinking how sorry she is that she broke her mother's vase? You may assume she isn't sorry, but maybe she is.

Sometimes you impose how you would react to a situation onto your child, when, in reality, she may be thinking something totally different. When children are young, they may be confused because they believe their parents must be right, yet what you say they're thinking is not at all what is in their heads. Variations of this include "I know you may be angry at me for this" and "All you think about is how to get what you want." It's important for children to know that they are separate from you and to understand that you cannot read their minds.

Fortune-Telling

"You'll never amount to anything," "It won't work," and "You'll be sorry"—these all are ways parents predict the future. Fortune-telling can be positive in nature as well: "You've made the right choice," or "That will work out perfectly." Right or wrong, positive or negative, you cannot predict an outcome. You can't really predict behavior based on past behavior, either.

Emotional Reasoning

This distortion differs from the others in that it is triggered by feelings instead of thoughts: *I feel it, so it must be true.* This is when you fear that your child is lying to you, so you think it must be true. Or you feel sad imagining that your child won't be able to handle being away overnight, so it must be true. Or you feel worried about your child's health, so there must be something wrong. Emotional reasoning starts with the feeling, from which the thought follows.

Personalization

Personalization is when you see events unrelated to you as being about you in a distorted way. When you believe that your child was purposely not getting ready on time to make you late for work, that probably means you have personalized the situation. Believing that your child talked back to you in front of a neighbor just to embarrass you would be another example.

Personalization means that you believe another person's behavior is strictly about you, and in this sense, it can be destructive in relationships and can interfere with validation.

Some Ways to Work with Your Cognitive Distortions

Spend some time identifying your own cognitive distortions. Sometimes being aware of them is sufficient for you to change them. Try writing them down each day in your notebook. Do you notice a pattern?

Another way to change cognitive distortions is to examine them carefully to understand what's true and what isn't. The following exercise is one way to do this. Write down your responses in your notebook; don't just answer in your head. The more thorough your answers, the more the exercise will benefit you.

Exercise 8.2   Dispute and Replace Cognitive Distortions

List the cognitive distortion that you want to address. Make it specific, such as "My eleven-year-old son is always in a bad mood when he comes home from school."

Note ways in which the statement is true. Be specific about how many times, say in a week, it is truly accurate.

Note ways in which that statement is not true.

Note ways that you would act toward your child based on that belief. Write how that affects your child and you.

What is the truth? This is your new statement.

Write how you would act with your child based on the new statement.

List how that would affect you and your child.

Check It Out

Another way to challenge cognitive distortions is to check them out with other people. Ask at least two trusted loved ones if they believe the statement you are addressing. Listen to their responses without discounting them.

Look for the Evidence

Because you may feel that something is true when it isn't, checking out the evidence is a good way to know what the truth is. If you believe that your son is always in a bad mood when he comes home from school, then mark the calendar. Mark the calendar every day for three weeks and then look at the results. How many days was he in a bad mood? If the thought is true that he is most often in a bad mood when he comes home from school, then you may need to do some problem solving. If he is in a bad mood only one or two days, then the belief is not true.

Other Issues That Get in the Way of Your Success

Part of being successful is knowing what might get in your way and having a plan to deal with those obstacles. To help you understand what your obstacles are, we thought it might be helpful to discuss some of the most common obstacles to validating parenting. You may find others along the way, and it may even be helpful for you to write them down and watch out for them as you grow in this process. Keep in mind that we mean to encourage you, not discourage you. What you know about yourself as a parent often helps you to see what you need to change.

Perfectionism

Sometimes you may set your expectations of yourself too high. Do you want to be a perfect parent who never loses composure and always makes the best choices? That wish to be the perfect parent may get in the way of acknowledging your mistakes. Perfectionism is paralyzing. Accepting your own vulnerabilities and mistakes may be too painful when your greatest fear is that of not being a good parent. Lowering your expectations of yourself may seem like an admission of failure. The truth is you are human. Even if you are conscious of the importance of self-care, there will be days when you have a headache, didn't get enough sleep, or are worried about your own mother's health. When you are physically ill or fatigued, or haven't been eating right or taking care of yourself, you will be vulnerable to acting impulsively and emotionally. On those days, you won't be able to function as well or do as much as you normally do. While this seems self-evident, most of us do not adjust our expectations of ourselves. We try to accomplish as much as when we feel well and rested. We continue to push ourselves. Then we are even more likely to react to our children out of emotion, not wisdom.

Everybody has strengths and weaknesses, and good days and bad days. If we accept that we cannot be perfect, we will be more forgiving of ourselves and others. If we believe we must be perfect, then we are teaching our children the same. Aiming for perfection means that we will fail, feel like a failure, and be paralyzed by that result. If you aim for perfection, you cannot be successful.

Depression, Anxiety, Substance Abuse, and Other Emotional Disorders

Perhaps you are a parent who suffers from emotional disorders. When depression strikes, you may have difficulty being present for your child.

Getting out of bed may be all that you can do. If you're using illegal substances or drinking excessively, you cannot be present for your child. Emotional disorders will naturally interfere with your practicing validating parenting. We urge you to find an effective therapist to help you. This is critical for your children.

Figuring Out the Problem

Sometimes parents become upset and unable to validate their children, perhaps even invalidating them because they can't control their own emotions. Often times they may not even understand why. All parents have had the experience of deeply regretting something they said or did with their children and wanting to get past that parenting pitfall. It's normal to promise to do better and want to forget what happened, but not understanding how you got to that point makes it more difficult to prevent the same behavior from recurring and, thus, is a block to your success in using validating parenting. It may be that when you invalidate your children, you are always tired or hungry. Or it may almost always happen on days when you have a work deadline. Or maybe it's about a certain behavior in your children, such as telling you how wonderful someone else's mother is. One way to help you figure out the problem is to use chain analysis for parents.

Chain analysis is a behavior technique Marsha Linehan (1993) refined that helps you figure out what situations, actions, thoughts, and feelings lead to a certain result. Start with a behavior you regret, like raising your voice with your child. Let's call this a parenting pitfall. Think about what happened before the incident. What led up to the parenting pitfall? Consider things people might have said, phone calls you received, something you did, or all possibilities of what went through your mind.

In the following exercise, you will write down special circumstances that may have affected your behavior, such as getting insufficient sleep or being sick. Sometimes parents expect to function the same whether or not they've slept, eaten well, or been sick. The truth is that parents who are tired cannot expect to accomplish as much as when they aren't tired, and they will be more emotionally sensitive when they are tired.

Exercise 8.3 Learn from Parenting Pitfalls

What I wish I hadn't done or said:

Example: *Yelled at my ten-year-old for not cleaning his room.*

BEFORE THE PARENTING PITFALL:

1. What happened right before the parenting pitfall? What were your thoughts? What were your feelings?

Example: *I took laundry into my son's room, which was a mess, as usual. I thought how unappreciated I am and felt frustrated.*

2. What happened right before that? What were your thoughts? What were your feelings?

Example: *My husband called and said he was going bowling with friends instead of coming home. I felt overwhelmed.*

3. What happened right before that? What were your thoughts? What were your feelings?

Example: *I was tired, had a long day trying to potty-train my two-year-old. I thought I didn't have enough patience. I felt hopeless as a parent.*

4. What happened before that? What were your thoughts? What were your feelings?

Example: *I didn't want to potty-train my two-year-old; I didn't feel confident. I dreaded the day and felt sad.*

AFTER THE PARENTING PITFALL

1. What happened right after the parenting pitfall? What were your thoughts and feelings?

Example: *My ten-year-old cried. I was too harsh and felt guilty.*

2. What happened after that? What were your thoughts and feelings?

Example: *My ten-year-old wouldn't talk with me. He looked hurt. I thought I was an awful parent and felt ashamed.*

3. What happened after that? What were your thoughts and feelings?

Example: *I tried to be extra nice to make it up to him. I thought I owed it to him, so I let him play his video games longer than usual. I felt helpless as a mother.*

PAYOFF

Was there a payoff for your child from the parenting pitfall? (Did anything good happen?)

Example: *He got to play video games longer than usual. I let him get by with halfway cleaning his room because I felt so guilty.*

Was there a payoff for you?

Example: *My ten-year-old made an effort to clean his room. I released some of my anger and felt calmer.*

Was there a payoff for anyone else?

Example: *My husband got to go bowling. Because I feel guilty, I rarely ask for help and he doesn't do much around the house.*

BEHAVIOR AWARENESS

What one event guaranteed that the parenting pitfall would happen?

Example: *My husband calling to say he was going bowling.*

How did you learn the behavior in the parenting pitfall?

Example: *A lot of times, when I yell at my kids to do things, it works, and that's what my mother did.*

SPECIAL CIRCUMSTANCES

Was there anything out of the ordinary happening in your life? Any unusual stresses, including fatigue or illness? What about for your child?

Example: *I had the flu last week and still wasn't back to normal. I got behind last week while I was sick, and I hate being behind.*

SOLUTION

Use your previous answers to answer the following questions.

Behavior Awareness: What could you change about the event that guaranteed the parenting pitfall would happen or your reaction to that event that could result in a more effective parenting response? Does understanding how you learned the parenting pitfall behavior offer any ideas about what you need to change or how to change?

Example: *In the future I could tell my husband when I need his help. I could be more open about my needs. I tend to yell when my needs aren't met. I'm just doing what's easier for me to get results. I need a different way to get my son to clean his room.*

Behavior Links: Looking at the preceding links, what can you change in each link that would lead to effective parenting instead of parenting pitfalls in the future?

Example: *If I changed how critical I am of myself, I would not be as upset.*

Payoffs: Is there a better way to get the same positive results?

Example: *Give my son consequences, like no television or video games until his room is clean. For myself, tell my husband when I need help so I don't get so frustrated, or find a friend to vent to so I don't take it out on my son. When I'm feeling better, exercise could also help me release frustration.*

Special Circumstances: What can you change about the special circumstances or your reaction to them that would lead to more effective parenting?

Example: *I could try to do less when I'm not feeling well and be aware that I'm less patient when ill. I could get a babysitter more often. I could set up a behavior reward system and feel more confident as a parent.*

ROADBLOCKS

What would interfere with your following through with the preceding solution?

Example: *My pride. I think I should be able to do it all myself. Finances are too tight for a babysitter. My husband and son might not like changes. I'm too tired.*

SOLUTIONS FOR ROADBLOCKS

How can you effectively deal with the roadblocks so that you can be successful in carrying out your solution?

Example: *Accept that I can't do it all and that it doesn't mean I'm a failure. I can budget better and plan for nights out with my husband or friends. I can remember the long-term goal and not give in to complaints about the changes until we've had a chance to see how they work.*

When you've completed this exercise, make a plan to help you be more effective in the future from the information you wrote in the sections on roadblocks and solutions for dealing with them. The purpose of this exercise is to help you see how thoughts and behaviors lead to certain outcomes. If you seem to lose control of your emotions with your children when you are tired, then finding a way to get more rest is a top priority. If you react badly when your children say nice things about a friend's parent, then maybe you need to consider your cognitive distortions. Or perhaps you become overly angry with your children when you feel shame, like when you forget to bring food you promised to contribute to the bake sale. Once you know what the issue is, then you can develop a strategy for dealing with the issue in a different, more productive way. Review your plan daily or even more frequently. Track your progress. Give it some time. If you can't change the behavior, you might want to consult a professional counselor who can help you develop a strategy that works for you.

A Lack of Self-Validation

Parents need validation too. People don't outgrow the need for validation, and parenting is one of the most challenging roles you'll ever have. Hopefully you have someone in your life who accepts you; is honest with you; and lets you know that your thoughts, feelings, and behaviors are understandable. If you were validated as a child, then you may be able to self-validate already. If you grew up in an invalidating environment, then you probably tend to invalidate yourself. One of the consequences of living in an invalidating environment is that you internalize that invalidating environment so that it becomes a part of you (Linehan 1993) and begin to invalidate yourself: *How could I be so stupid?* or *I never do anything right, no matter how hard I try.* The same consequences follow, whether you invalidate yourself or someone else invalidates you. Constantly criticizing yourself can bring about anxiety, anger, and self-rejection, which will make it more difficult for you to manage your emotions and be able to validate your children. If you have been telling yourself *I'm a horrible parent for yelling at my children,* maybe substitute *Given that I grew up in a family that yelled at me, I am working on not yelling at my children, and I am doing better. I have a plan that is helping me yell even less than I do now.* Remember, validation is about the truth. Although yelling is undesirable, it doesn't make you a horrible parent. That's a cognitive distortion, an overgeneralization. And although passing such a judgement on yourself may feel warranted, the invalidating statement does not help change the behavior. There's a reason why cheerleaders don't yell, "Give it up, team, give it up! You're lousy, and you know it; just sit down!" Validating yourself focuses on the truth and doesn't throw you into a pit of self-hate. So if you don't have someone in your life who validates you, find someone. And practice self-validation every chance you get. It will be good practice for validating your child as well!

Another reason to self-validate is that children learn by watching you. You are a role model for your children; children can learn to validate themselves by seeing you validate yourself. Your children watch you and absorb lessons just by being with you. If you tell them it's okay to make mistakes, but then verbally chastise yourself when you make a mistake, the behavior sends a much stronger message than the words. If you say it's okay to feel sad but then personally avoid sadness by covering up the sadness with a smile and denying feeling it, your children will learn that it's not okay to feel sad. If you are crying but deny it to your children, you are sending the message that it's not okay to cry. So, part of validating children is being able to validate yourself, being able to accept your own humanness and feelings, and acknowledge your own internal experience without judging it in a negative way. If you're truly comfortable with self-validation, then your child will be too.

It may be that you are an emotionally intense person whose feelings trigger strong actions, such as yelling or being rude when you're upset. You cannot validate your child if you are yelling at her and reacting from your own emotions. Validation means being able to be genuine about your own emotions, not out of control, which means that you communicate that you feel upset, disappointed, or whatever the emotion is that you are experiencing. If your child breaks your most expensive and cherished vase by running in the house when she knew she wasn't supposed to do that, you will be angry and disappointed. Denying how you feel will invalidate her sense of your emotions and confuse her. She knows that the breaking of your vase upsets you. This is where you separate the behavior from the child. Instead of saying you are disappointed in her, tell her you are disappointed that your vase is broken and disappointed that she broke the rule against running inside the house. You may need to get more in control of your own feelings before talking with her. It's okay to let her know that you need some time.

Lack of Understanding of Developmental Behaviors

Understanding the development timetable helps you validate the changes your child is going through. You don't have to read about the stages of development; paying attention to what your child says and does may help you understand what is developmentally normal. However, a series of books on child development from the Gesell Institute of Human Development may be helpful. These books offer rough, informative guidelines, although every child is different. For example, seven-year-olds (Bates Ames and Chase Haber 1987) can be more anxious and withdrawn at times than six-year-olds (Bates Ames and Ilg 1979), tend to feel picked on by others, and often worry that no one likes them. At eight, some children tend to become outgoing again, love talking, and be very aware of relationships. They tend to be critical of themselves and others and have a lot of self-doubt, and they can be quite dramatic in their reactions. From nine to eleven, children's fears are focused on realistic events rather than fantasy concerns. Nine-year-olds love to collect, tend to complain and worry, and make excuses (Bates Ames and Chase Haber 1991). Ten-year-olds tend to be confident and have more competitive relationships at school, eleven-year-olds can be less confident, and twelve-year-olds can be moody and unpredictable (Bates Ames, Ilg, and Baker 1988).

Understanding what are normal developmental characteristics can help you validate normalcy for your children and help ease your own concerns about changes your child goes through as she grows and matures.

Wrapping Up

This chapter discussed possible obstacles to using validating parenting successfully, including cognitive distortions, not wanting to look at your children's weaknesses, being unable to manage your emotions, suffering from emotional disorders, invalidating yourself, being perfectionistic, feeling shame, and not enjoying being a parent. We offered suggestions for working with these barriers to success.

Conclusion

Finally, we would like to thank you for taking the time to read our book. If it was not evident in the text and stories, we are passionate and believe very emphatically that applying these concepts to your daily parenting will make a difference.

We hope that you have gained a better sense of what validation is, why it is important, and how to apply it. We have seen so many relationships transformed by applying this concept to parenting and we believe that you will too.

We wish you the best in your parenting and in all of your relationships.

References

Ainsworth, M., M. Blehar, E. Waters, and S. Wall. 1978. *Patterns of Attachment*. Hillsdale, NS: Erlbaum.

Allen, K. E., and L. R. Marotz. 2003. *Developmental Profiles: Pre-Birth through Twelve*. 4th ed. Clifton Park, NY: Delmar Learning.

Bates Ames, L., and C. Chase Haber. 1987. *Your Seven-Year-Old: Life in a Minor Key*. New York: Dell.

———. 1990. *Your Eight-Year-Old: Lively and Outgoing*. New York: Dell.

———. 1991. *Your Nine-Year-Old: Thoughtful and Mysterious*. New York: Dell.

Bates Ames, L., and F. L. Ilg. 1979. *Your Six-Year-Old: Loving and Defiant*. New York: Dell.

Bates Ames, L., F. L. Ilg, and S. M. Baker. 1988. *Your Ten- to Fourteen-Year-Old*. New York: Dell.

Bernet, C. Z., R. E. Ingram, and B. R. Johnson. 1993. "Self-Esteem." In *Symptoms of Depression*, edited by C. G. Costello, 141–59. New York: Wiley.

Bradberry, T., and J. Greaves. 2009. *Emotional Intelligence 2.0.* San Diego, CA: TalentSmart.

Brown, B. 2007. *I Thought It Was Just Me (but It Isn't): Telling the Truth about Perfectionism, Inadequacy, and Power.* New York: Gotham Books.

Chess, S., and A. Thomas. 1986. *Temperament in Clinical Practice.* New York: The Guilford Press.

Doran, G. T. 1981. "There's a S.M.A.R.T. Way to Write Management's Goals and Objectives." *Management Review* 70 (11):35–36.

Ellis, A., and R. A. Harper. 1975. *A Guide to Rational Living.* 3rd ed. Chatsworth, CA: Wilshire Book Company.

Erikson, E. H. 1994. *Identity and the Life Cycle.* New York: W. W. Norton and Company.

Fulghum, R. 2004. *All I Really Need to Know I Learned in Kindergarten.* New York: Ballantine Books.

Gilbert, P. 2009. *The Compassionate Mind.* London: Constable and Robinson Ltd.

Gottman, J. 1997. *Raising an Emotionally Intelligent Child.* With J. DeClaire. New York: Simon and Schuster.

Gottman, J. M., L. Fainsilber Katz, and C. Hooven. 1997. *Meta-Emotion: How Families Communicate Emotionally.* Mahwah, NJ: Lawrence Earlbaum Associates.

Holmes, J. 1993. *John Bowlby and Attachment Theory.* New York: Routledge.

James, W. 1890. *Principles of Psychology.* Vol. 1. New York: Henry Holt and Company.

Janoff-Bulman, R., and P. Brickman. 1982. "Expectations and What People Learn from Failure." In *Expectations and Actions: Expectancy-Value Models in Psychology*, edited by N. T. Feather, 207–37. Hillsdale, NJ: Lawrence Erlbaum Associates.

Kabat-Zinn, J. 1990. *Full Catastrophe Living: Using the Wisdom of Your Body and Mind to Face Stress, Pain, and Illness.* New York: Delacorte Press.

———. 1994. *Wherever You Go, There You Are: Mindfulness Meditation in Everyday Life.* New York: Hyperion.

Karen, R. 1994. *Becoming Attached: Unfolding the Mystery of the Infant-Mother Bond and Its Impact on Later Life.* New York: Warner Books.

Kaufman, G. 1992. *Shame: The Power of Caring.* Rochester, VT: Schenkman Books.

Leahy, R. L. 2005. *The Worry Cure: Seven Steps to Stop Worry from Stopping You.* New York: Three Rivers Press.

Leary, M. R., R. M. Kowalski, L. Smith, and S. Phillips. 2003. "Teasing, Rejection, and Violence: Case Studies of the School Shootings." *Aggressive Behavior* 29 (3):202–14. doi:10.1002/ab.10061.

Lefcourt, H. M. 1976. *Locus of Control: Current Trends in Theory and Research.* Hillsdale, NJ: Lawrence Erlbaum Associates.

Linehan, M. M. 1993. *Cognitive Behavioral Treatment of Borderline Personality Disorder.* New York: The Guilford Press.

———. 1997. "Validation and Psychotherapy." In *Empathy Reconsidered: New Directions in Psychotherapy*, edited by A. C. Bohart and L. S. Greenberg, 353–92. Washington, DC: American Psychological Association.

Mogel, W. 2001. *The Blessing of a Skinned Knee: Using Jewish Teachings to Raise Self-Reliant Children.* New York: Scribner.

National Institute of Mental Health (NIMH). 2010. "Teenage Brain: A Work in Progress (Fact Sheet)." NIH Publication No. 01-4929. http.nimh.nih.

gov/health/publications/teenage-brain-a-work-in-progress-fact-sheet/ index.shtml (accessed April 4, 2011).

Packard, E. 2007. "That Teenage Feeling: Harvard Researchers May Have Found Biological Clues to Quirky Adolescent Behavior." *American Psychological Association Monitor* 38 (4):20.

Price Tangney, J., and R. L. Dearing. 2002. *Shame and Guilt*. New York: The Guilford Press.

Prochaska, J. O., J. C. Norcross, and C. C. DiClemente. 1994. *Changing for Good: The Revolutionary Program That Explains the Six Stages of Change and Teaches You How to Free Yourself from Bad Habits*. New York: William Morrow and Company.

Rogers, C. R. 1995. *On Becoming a Person: A Therapist's View of Psychotherapy*. Introduction by P. D. Kramer. New York: Mariner Books.

Rotter, J. B. 1966. "Generalized Expectancies for Internal versus External Control of Reinforcement." *Psychological Monographs* 80 (1):1–28.

Sadock, B. J., and V. A. Sadock. 2007. *Kaplan and Sadock's Synopsis of Psychiatry*. 10th ed. Philadelphia: Lippincott, Williams & Wilkins.

Seligman, M. E. P. 2002. *Authentic Happiness: Using the New Positive Psychology to Realize Your Potential for Lasting Fulfillment*. New York: The Free Press.

———. 2006. *Learned Optimism: How to Change Your Mind and Your Life*. New York: Vintage Books.

Siegel, D. J. 1999. *The Developing Mind: How Relationships and the Brain Interact to Shape Who We Are*. New York: The Guilford Press.

Stevenson, H. W. 1993. "Why Asian Students Still Outdistance Americans." *Educational Leadership* 50 (5):63–65.

Winnicott, D. W. 1992. *The Child, the Family, and the Outside World*. Cambridge, MA: De Capo Press.

Zastrow, C., and K. K. Kirst-Ashman. 2010. *Understanding Human Behavior and the Social Environment*. 8th ed. Belmont, CA: Brooks/Cole.

Errata

On page 157, Melissa H. Cook's photograph appears next to the biographical sketch for Karyn D. Hall, and vice versa. The Publisher regrets the error.

Photo by Al Torres Photography

Karyn D. Hall, PhD, is director and owner of the Dialectical Behavior Therapy Center in Houston, TX, and is an advisor, consultant, and trainer with Treatment Implementation Collaborative, LLC. Trained as a child psychologist, she specializes in the prevention and treatment of emotional disorders. Hall works with a dialectical behavior therapy team in Houston, TX, which generously enriches her professional endeavors and offers wisdom on a daily basis.

Photo by Evin Thayer

Melissa H. Cook, LPC, has been intensively trained in dialectical behavior therapy (DBT) and validation, and owns a private practice in Houston, TX. She is a renowned speaker on these topics and utilizes the principles of DBT and validation both as a therapist and a mother of three. Cook struggled with and recovered from anorexia and has since dedicated her life to helping others. She lives in Houston, TX, with her children, Stuart, David, and Caroline, and her husband, Douglas, to whom she has been married for over seventeen years.

Foreword writer **Shari Y. Manning, PhD,** is a founder and chief executive officer of Treatment Implementation Collaborative, LLC. She is author of *Loving Someone with Borderline Personality Disorder.*

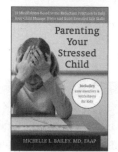

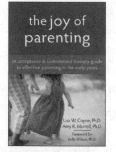